IT Glossary
for schools

IT Glossary
for schools

Compiled by
The British Computer Society Schools Committee
Glossary Working Party

Members of the working party

Arnold Burdett

Diana Burkhardt

Aline Cumming

John Cushion

Alan Hunter

Frank Hurvid

John Jaworski

Tim Reeve (Chairman)

Graham Rogers

John Southall

 LONGMAN

on behalf of the British Computer Society

Pearson Education Limited
Edinburgh Gate, Harlow
Essex CM20 2JE, England
and Associated Companies throughout the world

First published 1997
Second impression 1999
Third impression 1999

British Library Cataloguing in Publication Data
A catalogue entry for this title is available from the British Library

ISBN 0-582-31255-8

Printed in Malaysia, PA

Contents

How to use this glossary

All definitions are preceded by a **bold heading**. Each term which is defined appears in the index.

Some definitions include other related terms. These terms are listed in a line of *italic print* after the main heading and are printed in ***bold italic*** type in the text of the definition. Sometimes there are alternate terms with the same meaning, these are also listed in an *italic line* and all index entries give the page number of the main heading.

For example, in section A6 on page 30, the definition of 'Graphics tablet' includes the definitions of the terms *Stylus* and *Puck* and contains the alternative term 'graphics pad':

Graphics tablet
also known as: graphics pad
including: stylus, puck
is a device used to input line drawings into a computer. The user draws with a *stylus* on a flat pad or tablet (sometimes called a ***graphics pad***), either copying a drawing or working freehand.

Stylus is the name for devices used for drawing on a graphics tablet. The movement of the stylus is detected by the tablet and its software in one of a variety of ways, for example through the use of a wire matrix in the pad or by sensing the angular movement of an arm supporting the stylus. A stylus may be pressure sensitive, producing a darker or more intensely coloured line if pressed firmly.
Puck is a small disk-shaped device, which is moved around on the tablet (or pad) to trace a drawing.

The position of the stylus or puck on the tablet is input to the computer and used to position a cursor on the screen. Subsequent movement causes a drawing on the screen which matches the movements on the tablet. These devices are generally preferred to a mouse for computer drafting packages.

Terms that are being referenced are put in italics to highlight them and an indication is given about where to find them. For example, '**digitiser**' on page 30 includes in its text:

A digitiser scans a drawing and turns it into a *bit map* (see below);

'(see above)' or '(see below)' are used when the term is to be found in the same section, otherwise a page number is given. This page number will be the number of the page on which the referenced term is defined.

Introduction

IT glossary comprises a selection of terms from **A glossary of computing terms** 8th edition, 1995. The terms contained in this selection are generally appropriate for work at Key Stage 4. They are suitable for use in both Information Technology courses and the general curriculum in schools. Students following other courses, such as NVQ level 1 or 2 courses with an IT component, may find much of the material in this glossary useful. The terms omitted from the 8th edition for this present volume are mostly appropriate to post-16 advanced courses. Many students and teachers following computer-based courses at school, college and university welcome the full spectrum of terms as provided by the full 8th edition.

It is appropriate to mention that the glossary was originally produced as the result of a request in 1974 by the Regional Examinations Boards (for schools) to the British Computer Society for a standardised list of terms to be used in the emerging computer studies courses in schools. The early editions proved so popular that they were widely used in schools, colleges, universities and industrial training departments, on a variety of courses featuring the application of computers.

————— ~ —————

The Working Party would welcome offers from teachers willing to involve their students in a review of this edition. Comments on this edition and contributions or suggestions for future editions will be gratefully received and should be sent to the Chair of the working party via The Education Department, BCS, 1 Sanford Street, Swindon SN1 1HJ.

Part A:
How Computer Systems Are Used

This section contains terms which may be met by any computer user working with applications in any of the areas covered. Some sections in Part A are concerned with general issues and others with well defined areas of computer use. Some sections contain terms which might have been placed in Part B but they were kept with other related terms for completeness; this is particularly true of the sections covering sound and user interfaces, which have become more prominent aspects of computer use since the previous edition was published. Some terms have references to terms in Part B which will provide readers with pointers to other associated terms and concepts.

A1 Data Processing (DP)

Other concepts related to the design and implementation of systems to carry out commercial data processing are found in several later sections, especially B8 Systems Design and Development, B9 System Documentation and B11 Data Representation and Management.

Data Processing in its broadest – and technically correct – sense covers every task which a computer carries out. Traditionally its meaning has been restricted to those particular computing applications and activities concerned with business and commerce.

The term has tended not to be used when describing the processing of scientific data where complex mathematical calculations are performed. In many business applications, relatively straight-forward tasks are carried out on relatively small amounts of data for each transaction but repeated routinely for each of a very large number of individual records in the same run. Typical of such application areas are accounting, payroll, record keeping, route planning, stock control. Nevertheless, with business operations becoming more complex – particularly where large-scale modelling is involved – the dividing line between business and scientific processing is not so clear-cut as it previously appeared. In addition to its meaning as an operation, 'data processing' is also used as the title of the section of an organisation which carries out this area of work.

The user organisations typically associated with these traditional data processing applications are banks, government departments and a whole range of businesses. For any particular application type (for example, payroll), there is often a standard type of package, although there may be many variations of it available. Also, although all users will need to use a particular type of package to do the same job, they may require a specific version because they have different hardware or operating systems or because they need to use the package in association with another application area.

Associated with this area of computing are particular programming languages (**COBOL** is a prime example) and techniques (for example, database management).

Within most commercial organisations there will be a Data Processing Manager and a small team of support staff who will have overall responsibility for seeing that the system provides a satisfactory service to the users (individuals or departments). However, the individual departmental users are responsible for defining those data processing tasks which the system is required to carry out for them, while the maintenance of all the system – hardware and software – is likely to be done on contract by outside people.

Article number

including: ISBN, UPC, EAN

is the number given to a particular product (for example, the *International Standard Book Numbers (ISBN)* found on a book). This is often printed together with its bar-code representation, so that it can be read both by people and automatically by a *wand* (see page 107) or some other *point-of-sale terminal* device (see page 150). The numbers are usually structured, and there are international agreements on how the numbers should be constructed for various types of goods. Two common forms of numbering system are the *Universal Product Code (UPC)* and the *European Article Number (EAN)*.

Audit trail

is a record of the file updating that takes place during a specific transaction. It enables a trace to be kept of all operations on files.

Bar code

is a pattern of parallel black-and-white lines used to represent a code number, which can then be read automatically. It is often used by shops to identify a product at the cash-desk so that its price can be found automatically from a computer, as an alternative to a cash-till operator entering the price directly through a keypad.

Computer Bureau

is an organisation which offers a range of computing services for hire (for example, data preparation, payroll processing). Bureaux usually offer two types of service: they provide computing facilities for organisations which do not have any of their own and they also offer specialist services covering vital common operations (for example, payroll) to organisations which do not have the appropriate piece of applications software.

Control total

is the sum resulting from the addition of a specified field from each of a group of records, for example adding tax deductions in a payroll program. It is used for checking data.

Data capture

is the action of collecting data for use in a particular computer process. This may be done automatically, as in the continuous monitoring of temperature in a chemical process, or manually as in gas meter reading. See also *data capture* in A9 Control, page 39.

Data preparation

is the translation of data into machine-readable form.

Direct Data Entry (DDE)

is the input of data for batch processing using a key-to-disk unit. The data may be validated while held in a temporary file before being written to the disk for subsequent processing.

Encryption

is the technique of encoding data to make it meaningless to those who do not know how to decode it. See also *encryption* in A18 Law and Administration, page 96.

File

in data processing, is an organised collection of related records, see also *file*, page 179.

Grandfather, father, son files

are the three most recent versions of a file that is periodically updated. They are retained for security purposes.

Information

is the meaning given to structured data by the context in which it is interpreted.

Information processing

is the organisation, manipulation and distribution of information. As these activities are central to almost every use of computers, the term is in common use to mean almost the same as 'computing'.

Information technology (IT)

is the application of appropriate (enabling) technologies to information processing. The current interest centres on computing, telecommunications and digital electronics.

Kimball tag
is a small punched card attached to merchandise, which is detached when goods are sold, to provide machine-readable sales data.

Master file
is a file of data which is a principal source of information for a job. It can be updated or amended as necessary. In a batch processing system a *transaction file* (see below) is used to update the master file.

Transaction file
also known as: update file, changes file
is a collection of records used in batch processing to update a *master file* (see above).

Turnaround document
is a document that, after being output by the computer, can be used to record additional data. All the data from that completed document can then in turn be input to the computer.

Validation
including: data vetting
is the checking, by the computer, of data at the input stage to detect any data that is incomplete or unreasonable. Methods used include *check digits*, *range checks* (see below) and *data types* (see below). It is also known as ***data vetting***.

Data verification
including: verifier
is the act of checking transferred data − usually at the stage of input to a computer − by comparing copies of the data before and after transfer (for example, repeating the keyboard operations to check that the data has been correctly transferred in a key-to-disk system). Where a separate device performs this task, it is called a ***verifier***. Other methods, such as *control totals* (see above) and *hash totals* (see below), operate on batches of data.

Management Information Systems (MIS)
are designed to provide small amounts of management-level information − such as summaries of the larger amounts of data which individual user departments might require. This type of information may typically be used by managers as an aid to monitoring budgets or assessing sales targets.

Decision Support Systems (DSS)

are refined *management information systems* (see above) where the emphasis
is on providing senior management with key information for strategic decision
making. Such systems use sophisticated analysis techniques and may include
expert systems (see page 68).

Archive file

is a file containing data that is no longer in current use but which must be kept
in long-term storage as it may be required at some future date, for example
certain accounts information required for audit purposes. For security
reasons, archive files are usually kept away from the computer system to
which they belong.

Backup file

is a copy of a file, to be available in the event of the original file being
corrupted or lost.

Check digit

is an extra digit, or other character, derived from the original digits (usually by
summing these in a number base which is different to that of the actual
number). It is then attached to the original number as a means of later
checking its validity.

Hash total

including: check sum
is a control total, which has no external meaning, for example in a payroll
program the sum of the employee numbers. Also known as a *check sum*.

Hashing

is the process of generating a number, usually by some calculation on the
values in a field, record or area of store regardless of their meaning. This
number could then be used as a *hash total* (see above), as a position in a table,
a position on a disk, etc.

Range check

is a validation method where the data is rejected if its value is outside specified
limits.

Reference file

is a special type of master file which during normal use is read-only and is used to contain data which does not normally change. A special program would be used when the data needs altering. An example is the 'price file' in a supermarket point-of-sale system: the computer finds out the cost of each item sold during the day, but the file is only updated when prices change perhaps once a day or once a week.

Data type

including: alphanumeric data, string data, numeric data, integer data, real data, binary data, logical (or Boolean) data, sample data, sound data, video data, video clip, date data

is a formal description of the kind of data being stored or manipulated by a system. Examples of the more important data types that may be available include:

Alphanumeric data is a general term used for textual data which may include letters, digits and, sometimes, punctuation. It includes both *character data,* see page 178, or *string data,* which is textual data in the form of a list of characters, for example words and punctuation.

Numeric data is a general term used for data which consists of numbers. It includes a variety of number forms such as *integer data* (positive or negative whole numbers), *real data* (numbers, such as decimals, which include a fractional part). See also *numeric display format*, page 48 and *numeric data*, page 178.

Binary data consists of numbers and uses only the digits 0 and 1 (the base 2 number system). It is a convenient way of representing numbers in an electronic computer. Most computers perform arithmetic using binary numbers and convert the results to other forms for display.

Logical data or *Boolean data* can only have one of two values, *true* or *false*. This makes it easy to use the values of Boolean variables to control the flow of a program.

Sample data (digitally recorded *sound data*) and *video data* (a *video clip*) are large complex data structures containing all the information needed to enable a suitable system to play a sound sample or display a video clip.

Date data is in a form recognised as representing a date, for example 03/05/92 or 1st February 1995 are acceptable formats. Date data must represent a valid date, for example 11/12/84 is allowed, but 31st April 1995 or 31/4/95 are not.

A2   *Word Processing (WP)*

For details of printing and display devices used in word and document processing applications, see sections B4 Display Devices and B5 Printers.

Word Processing is the application of computing to the editing, formatting and production of typed letters and documents, including the addition of stored text (for example, for personalised circulars). A system dedicated to this application is often referred to as a **word processor**. An alternative to a word processor when only very limited formatting is needed is a text editor.

Document Processing is an extension of the formatting functions which have been common to word-processing packages for some years, in order to allow the integration of non-textual characters into the layout. Associated with this extension has been the use of bit-mapping or pixel mapping to take advantage of the ability of extremely high definition monitors and of laser-printer techniques to produce fine lines, graduated density and (where necessary) apparently continuous spectrum colour.

Typical document production will include diagrams, graphic characters, numeric, picture representation and symbols as well as text. The software associated with Document Processing needs to be able to manipulate areas of the document as if it were a single entity – analogous to alphanumeric character manipulation in text processing.

A general requirement of computers which run document processing systems is an abundance of memory and a fast processor.

Cut & paste

including: clipboard, notepad

is the technique of transferring a section of data (text in a word processor, or diagrams and text in a page make-up package) from one part of a document to another part of the same document, or to another document. In some systems the data is held in a temporary storage area called the *clipboard* or *notepad*. Data held in these storage areas will normally remain there until overwritten by new data, so allowing one exact copy of the original to be pasted in more than one place.

Dictionary
is the list of allowable words which can be used in a particular application.
Although most applications contain a standard dictionary, sometimes there is a
facility to allow an individual user to create a separate personal dictionary
which is then referred to if a particular word entered by that user is not found
in the standard dictionary.

Desk-top presentation
is the use of graphics, charting and page make-up software, together with high-
quality output devices, to produce sophisticated information displays. These
will normally be seen on screen or printed out onto paper. However, using
specialised devices, the information can also be output directly to overhead
projector foil, onto photographic film to provide high-quality slides or even
projected directly onto a cinema-style screen, for use in lectures and
demonstrations.

Desk-Top Publishing (DTP)
is the use of a *page make-up system* (see below) and high-quality output
devices to produce material which can be used directly as the first stage in the
production process for printed leaflets, manuals, books, magazines, reports,
etc.

Export
including: import
is to create a file using one piece of software so that it can be read by a
different piece of software. *Import* is the corresponding read process to accept
a file produced by some other software. Often there is a specific version of a
particular package whose file and data formats are chosen by its manufacturer
to be the standard version for exporting from and importing into that package.
    Using these formats reduces the problems of data transfer between different
software applications.

Hard space
including: soft space
is intended space that the user has explicitly typed (such as the space between
two adjacent words). *Soft space* is inserted by software to even out the look
of a line in order to create justified text. Because the user may later alter the
formatting of the text, these 'extra' spaces must be remembered by the
software, so that they can be removed where necessary. Reformatting justified
text does not remove hard spaces.

Justification

including: left justification, right justification, full justification, centring
is the arrangement of characters so that they align with margins. This may
occur on the screen or on a printer, or may be required when setting out data in
columns or as forms.

Left justification is the normal method of aligning
continuous text, with an even left-hand margin. This
often leaves an uneven right-hand margin since each
printed line is likely to contain characters (for
words, spaces and punctuation marks) which occupy
different lengths of line.

  Right justification is normal for columns of numbers,
   although it is sometimes seen in text. Here, an even
  right-hand margin is created. This may well result in
  a ragged left-hand margin, since each printed line is
    likely to contain characters (for words, spaces and
  punctuation) which occupy different lengths of line.

Full justification (sometimes simply referred to as
justification) has even margins at both left-hand and
right-hand ends of the line. It is created by the
(automatic) insertion of extra spaces (soft spaces)
between words once a line of approximately the correct
length has been entered.

Centring,
which is often used for headings
and
similar displays,
places the characters symmetrically between the
margins.

Figure A2.1: Different justification styles

Line break

is the place where a line of printed text ends. Word processors normally break
lines only between words or, if sufficiently sophisticated, by inserting hyphens
at appropriate places.

Mailmerge

is the process of combining a document (often a letter), and a data file (often a
list of names and addresses), in such a way that copies of the document for
different people are suitably different. In its simplest form, this is merely
ensuring that letters have the correct style and title for the addressee and that

the address is inserted into the appropriate place. More complex uses can include inserting whole paragraphs into standard letters or documents. The process remains the same for all applications; a document is set up which has marked places within it at which data from other files is inserted.

Micro-spacing

is a feature available on some printers to print fully justified text by inserting small amounts of *soft space* (see above) in order to spread the total amount of added space evenly across a line. This ability is particularly necessary when proportional fonts (where characters occupy different widths of printed space) are being used and fully justified text is still required.

Non-breaking space
including: pad character

is the type of space (such as that in "Henry IV") which occurs between words that should not appear on separate lines. Many word processors allow the user to type a special combination of keys to insert such a character, sometimes called a *pad character*, which will print as a space, but will not be allowed as a line break.

Overtype
sometimes: overwrite

is to replace text on a screen with other text entered from the keyboard (or possibly read from a file) during the process of entering or editing a document.

Page make-up system

allows on-screen combination of graphics and text. The software allows easy manipulation of the layout to produce a professional-looking result that can be reproduced for leaflets, manuals, magazines, etc.

Spelling checker

is a program which is normally used with a word processor or desk-top publishing system to check the spelling in a document. Each word in the document is checked against the *dictionary* (see above). If it does not appear in the dictionary then the user is told this. The word may be correct (but not in the dictionary) or it may be wrongly spelt. Some programs even check the spelling as the document is typed in.

TeX

including: Latex, Metafont

is a specialised text processing system devised by the American mathematician and computer scientist Donald Knuth. It allows much greater control over the display of mathematical and scientific formulas than conventional word processors and is often used by academic authors submitting technical manuscripts to journal or book publishers. The power of TeX makes it a difficult language for beginners, and a number of alternative user interfaces, such as *Latex*, have been designed – this offers the facilities for the production of a number of common types of scientific document without the user needing to write pure TeX. As well as the text-processing features of these languages, there is an associated type-face definition system called *Metafont*.

Text editor

is a program for creating and amending text. It is designed to be used for preparing the source text of programs and for editing text files. It can have similar editing functions to a word processor but requires a more formal approach than is usual in word processing if formatting is to be retained.

Thesaurus

is a dictionary arranged by meaning instead of spelling. A computer-based thesaurus used in conjunction with a word processor allows a user to select a word in the text, and to be offered a range of words with similar or related meanings. Using one of these instead of the original word can enhance the writer's prose style.

Word wrap

is a facility available in many word processing packages which breaks lines automatically between words. When the text being typed on the line reaches beyond the right-hand margin, the whole of the last word is transferred to the beginning of the next line.

WYSIWYG (What You See Is What You Get)

(pronounced 'wizzy-wig') refers to a screen display which matches the eventual printed output in layout, highlighting and underlining, font, etc. Such displays are particularly helpful in applications such as *desk-top publishing* (see above) and *spreadsheets* (see A3, page 13).

A3 Spreadsheets

Spreadsheets are an important and powerful use of the computer. A spreadsheet is based on the idea of the computer looking like a large sheet of squared paper with the added advantage of being able to do arithmetic.

	A	B	C	D	E	F	G	H	I
1									
2									
3									
4									
5						hello			
6									
7									
8									
9									

Figure A3.1: A spreadsheet

The squares are usually called cells (sometimes slots) and each is identified by its column label (often a letter or letters) and its row label (often a number). In the example the cell with hello in it has address F5, where F is the column label and 5 is the row label. The contents of a cell may be one of several types:

- a heading or message;
  this is just plain text - i.e. a collection of characters.
- a number;
  it is important to realise that there is a difference between a number as text and a number that is required for calculation – most spreadsheets allow for the conversion between a number as text and a number in a form suitable for calculation.
- a formula that represents a calculation;
  in this case what is seen in the cell is the result of the calculation rather than the formula itself. An example of a formula may be one that adds the contents of two cells together and multiplies the result by 3:

    3*(A21 + B21)

(If A21 contains the number 5 and B21 contains the number 6

then the cell containing the formula above will display the number 33. It still contains the formula after the calculation has been done, so that if the contents of A21 or B21 change then a new calculated value will be displayed.)

- an instruction;
  an example would be an instruction that takes the contents of a cell (a number) and uses it as a product code. The instruction then causes a table of product codes, prices and descriptions elsewhere in the table (or even possibly a different spreadsheet) to be searched and when the correct product code is found the description is inserted in the current cell which contains the instruction. In another cell would be an instruction to do the same but to insert the price.

Figure A3.2 is an example of a spreadsheet showing how many French francs one would get for different amounts of English money.

	A	B	C	D
1	Exchange Rate			
2	11.50	Pounds	Francs	
3		0	0.00	
4		5	57.50	
5		10	115.00	
6				

NOTE:
Cells C3, C4 and C5
each contain a
formula:
in C3 it is B3*A2
in C4 it is B4*A2
in C5 it is B5*A2

Figure A3.2: *A spreadsheet for currency conversion*

In this spreadsheet you can see numbers (for example, in cell B4), labels or headings (for example, in cell C2), and the result of applying a formula (as in cell C4). However, a spreadsheet need not be used for just doing the original calculation, it will also respond to changes in the data. It is this ability to respond to *'what if'* questions that makes a spreadsheet such a powerful business tool.

What if the rate of exchange altered? You can cope with this by simply re-typing the exchange rate in cell A2 and the freshly converted amounts of francs would appear in column C.

What if the amount of pounds that you wanted to exchange was not in the table? Type the amount in place of the zero amount in cell B3 and the converted amount will appear in cell C3.

In the above example the formulas used in column C are all very similar, but not quite identical; they all use A2 but this is multiplied by the appropriate entry in column B. On most spreadsheets there is no need to type each formula in individually: by replication you can repeat them automatically and make the system keep the reference to A2 every time but alter the reference to column B. Many spreadsheets also have a facility to take a set of figures and convert them into some type of graph (such as a pie chart, a line graph, or a bar chart).

The printing out of a spreadsheet can pose problems. Some software will just print out everything that is being used. However, most allow the user to indicate the cells that are to be printed out; many allow the cells to be printed out in a different order from their 'natural' one so that parts of the sheet that are separated by a lot of rows/columns can be printed close together. Some spreadsheets even allow the sheet to be printed sideways to allow for a wide sheet to be printed. A further complication in printing is what should be printed out for some of the cells - should it be a formula or the result of the formula? Again, many spreadsheets allow the user to choose.

The use of spreadsheets has been extended beyond just numbers. Imagine a list of names and addresses; each one might consist of (say) four entries: (a) the name, (b) the house number, (c) the road and (d) the town. Each entry could be put into a different column and each row hold a different name and address, as in Figure A3.3.

	A	B	C	D	E
1	Name	No.	Road	Town	
2	Mr Smith	1	Acacia Avenue	Birmingham	
3	Mrs Jones	2	High Street	Luton	
4	Ms Black	77	Sunset Road	Liverpool	
5	Miss World	12	Hillside	Leicester	
6					
7					

Figure A3.3: A spreadsheet used as a database

So you can use a spreadsheet as a simple database. Further to this, some spreadsheets can be used as word processors (in fact the draft of this text was prepared on such a spreadsheet). Usually this means that the text is set out in one column of the spreadsheet, but the other columns can be used as well. This becomes even more powerful when you wish to include some calculations in your text as there are no calculations for the user to do since the spreadsheet will do them all!

Cell

also known as: slot

including: address, column, row, block

is the 'square' on a spreadsheet in which only a single entry can be placed, sometimes called a *slot*. The single entry can be either a number, a group of words or a formula. It can be referred to by its *address* in the spreadsheet using the *column* and *row* labels. The column label refers to a vertical group of cells and the row label refers to a horizontal group of cells (see Figure A3.3). If we have a rectangular grouping of the cells this is termed a *block*. Usually the block is identified by giving the addresses of the upper left cell and the lower right cell of the rectangle, for example the block A3F12 would have 6 columns (A to F) of 10 rows (3 to 12).

Formula

is the way a calculation is represented in a spreadsheet. As well as numbers a formula uses the address of cells to identify other values to be used - the result is then displayed in the cell in which the formula was placed. If any of the cells referenced in the formula change in value then the result of the formula is changed to reflect the altered values.

For example, if the first side of a rectangle is in B3 and you wished to find the second side of the rectangle (in C3, say) whose sides always add up to (say) 12, the formula in C3 might be:

$$(12 - 2*B3)/2$$

Function

is a special type of formula used in a spreadsheet. It has usually been set up to represent a formula that may be too complex or too long to expect an ordinary user to enter, or it may be just very useful. Examples of this might be:

SUM()   a function to calculate the sum (i.e. the total) of a row or a column or a block of cells.

MEAN()   a function to calculate the average (mean) of a row or a column or a block of cells.

FIND()   a function to find where, in an area of the spreadsheet, a particular value is to be found.

Recalculation

is the term used to describe the process whereby the spreadsheet recalculates the values that may have altered because of the last input of data. The process of recalculation can be automatic - done after each and every entry in the spreadsheet - or it can be manual, whereby the user decides when it should be done and presses a particular set of keys to have the recalculation done. The advantage of having it set to manual is that the entry of data is quicker as the user does not have to wait for the updating (which can take an appreciable amount of time if the spreadsheet is large); the disadvantage is that the user has always to indicate when the recalculation should be done. It is sometimes important to know the order of the recalculation - whether it is by row (i.e. the first row, then the second and so on) or by column (i.e. the first column, then the second and so on). With many spreadsheets it is possible to alter the order of calculation.

Replication
including: absolute reference, relative reference

is the process of copying a formula from one cell to another. As a formula usually involves references to cells this means you should be aware of whether you want to keep the exact same reference to the cell (this is termed an *absolute reference*) or whether you want the reference to adjust itself according to either the row or column movement (this is termed a *relative reference*). An example of this is when you have a formula in cell A12 that calculates (say) the sum of a row of figures – something like SUM(A1...A10) – and this is then replicated into cell B12. Generally you will want the result to represent the sum for row B; if you tell it that A1 and A10 are relative then this will happen.

Spreadsheet

is an applications package usually used to display financial or statistical information. It takes its name from the way data is arranged on the screen in rows and columns, as in the traditional layout of figures in account books. The user can specify that numbers displayed in particular positions are to be dependent on entries in other positions, and are to be recalculated automatically when these entries are changed. Hence the effects of changes to one data item on, for example, totals, sub-totals, 'profits' and 'VAT' can be explored.

A4   *Communications*

Other related terms may be found in sections B6 Networks,
B7 Communications Devices and Control Devices.

The internal architecture of a computer involves electronic signals being
passed from component to component. It is a natural extension of this idea to
send signals *out* of the computer, to another computer, perhaps thousands of
kilometres away. Some of the technology used to achieve this is included in
section B7. On an electronic scale, the distance of a few metres to your printer
is so large that it raises a new set of problems (is the printer actually switched
on? – what does the computer do if it isn't?): these problems are surprisingly
not made *much* more severe if the printer is across the other side of the
Atlantic. So it seems quite natural for a number of computer applications to
have been developed that involve communication and information-provision
over large distances.

    Many of the applications have become so much a part of modern
industrialised societies that it takes us aback to realise that they involve
computing technology – taking cash from a cash dispenser in the middle of the
night in a strange town, sending a fax, reading the sports results on Teletext,
and so on.

Bulletin board

including: system operator (sysop), Campus 2000
is the electronic equivalent of a notice-board, carrying short items that may be
of interest to a wide number of people. Bulletin boards are sited on a
computer, and the users access the computer by a *network* (see page 144) or
electronic mail (see below). They can leave messages for anyone to read,
review messages left by other users and sometimes take copies of software that
has been placed on the board. The organiser of such a board is traditionally
known as the *system operator* or more familiarly as the *sysop*. Larger bulletin
boards are run by organisations such as newspapers, computer manufacturers
or universities, and offer comprehensive information services as well as an
opportunity to read or post messages. A popular large board accessed by
many schools because of its educational focus is *Campus 2000*.

Figure A4.1: A typical bulletin board screen

Cellular phone

is a portable radio-telephone that can be used while moving around (for example, in a car). The country is divided into overlapping cells, each a few miles in diameter and centred on a low-powered transmitter/receiver. When a call is made, it is handled by the nearest transmitter, but automatically switched to an adjacent cell (without a break in the call) if the handset moves out of range.

Computer conferencing

makes use of *electronic mail* (see below) to allow a group of people with a common interest, but geographically separated, to share advice, opinions, information and so on. The users are organised in a 'conference' and are able to examine messages left by other users, add their own comments, and generally participate in the work of the group. This is very similar to the idea of a *bulletin board* (see above), but there is a suggestion in a computer conference that users are all on an equal footing, and are all expected to contribute equally.

Computer-Supported Co-operative Work (CSCW)

including: work group

It is too early to tell whether this unwieldy description will find a permanent place in computer terminology: it describes the use of networked computer systems to enable **work groups** of employees to share documents, diaries and other computer files.

Closed User Group (CUG)

Not all information services on a *Viewdata* system (see below) are available to all subscribers. Commercial businesses, for example, may choose to provide information only to registered dealers or sales representatives: such a group is known as a 'closed' user group.

Electronic Funds Transfer (EFT)

including: debit card, EFTPOS, cash dispenser, automatic teller machine (ATM)

is the use of computer networks to transfer money. This may be done between banks, as an alternative to sending a cheque or a bankers' draft, especially where international transfers are involved. Most large companies now pay their employees by electronic transfer of funds into their personal bank accounts. Increasingly, it is being used in retail stores as an alternative to payment by credit card or cheque: the purchaser offers a *debit card* which is processed in the same way as a credit card, but which initiates the transfer of money from the purchaser's account directly to the shop's account. In this use, it is normally known by the cumbersome title of *Electronic Funds Transfer at Point-of-Sale (EFTPOS)*. The same principles are involved in a cash withdrawal from a *cash dispenser* or *automatic teller machine (ATM)*.

Electronic mail ('E-mail')

including: mailbox, JANET, Internet

is the sending of messages from user to user on a computer network. The message is stored in the recipient's *mailbox* until the next time that they use the computer, when they will be told that there is a message waiting, and can inspect it, print it out or reply. Because it is relatively cheap, and because the sender and the recipient do not both have to be using their computers at the same time, it is a popular way for schools and colleges to communicate with colleagues in other countries. There is an encouraging amount of international co-operation between the larger networks, which allows messages to be sent internationally through *gateways* (see page 152) between networks. The *Internet* is one such super-network. The principal academic network used for E-mail between British universities and colleges is *JANET (Joint Academic Network)*. Figure A4.2 shows how E-mail messages are passed, by describing the routing information that accompanies a typical message.

```
Date: Tue, 12 May 92 16:06:31
To: j_jaworski@open.ac.uk
From: linda_hof@ca.sfu
Subject: politics
```

Tuesday afternoon, 4.06pm Pacific Standard Time – Linda Hof sends a message about 'politics' from her terminal in Simon Fraser University in Canada ('ca.sfu') to John Jaworski in England: his E-mail address 'open.ac.uk' will allow the message to be routed to the UK, to the 'academic community', and finally to the Open University.

```
Received: from mpx8529.educ.sfu.ca by whistler.sfu.ca (5.65/SFU-2.0)
     id AA05341;
  Tue, 12 May 92 16:06:31
```

Linda is using the mpx8529 system in the education faculty. The message first goes to the main university computer, called 'whistler'; an identification number is attached to it.

```
Message-Id: <9205122306.AA05341@whistler.sfu.ca>
```

The Simon Fraser University computer adds some more identification to the message, so it can be traced back if it fails to be delivered correctly. This computer connects directly to the Internet which links it to the UK. The message is sent, split into small packets of data, and reassembled in the UK.

```
Received: from [128.189.32.1] by vax.NSFnet-Relay.AC.UK via NSFnet with SMTP
  id aa06724; 13 May 92 0:04 BST
```

Just after midnight, British Summer Time (about two minutes before it left, which means that somebody's clock was set badly!) the message arrives in the UK. [128.189.32.1] is the Internet identification of the Simon Fraser Computer on the network. The NSFnet-relay computer is the 'gateway' to the Internet for the UK

```
Received: from vax.nsfnet-relay.ac.uk by sun.nsfnet-relay.ac.uk
  with Internet SMTP id <sg.28177-3@sun.nsfnet-relay.ac.uk>;
  Wed, 13 May 1992 00:12:48 +0100
```

It is transferred from the gateway computer to a local Sun machine that will distribute the message in the UK – this takes about 8 minutes!

```
Via: UK.AC.NSFNET-RELAY; Wed, 13 May 92 0:15 GMT
```

And finally, about half an hour later, it arrives at the Open University computer; it will be in John Jaworski's mailbox when he next logs in.

```
From:   CBS%UK.AC.NSFNET-RELAY::CA.SFU::LINDA_HOF 13-MAY-1992
        00:15:13.24
To:     j_jaworski
CC:
Subj:   politics
```

Figure A4.2: *The life story of an E-mail message*

Facsimile transmission (Fax)

including: fax groups, junk fax
is the use of regular voice-quality telephone lines to send copies of documents, which may include drawings as well as text. The sender inserts the document into their own fax machine, and dials the receiving machine, which must be available at that time, and not busy sending or receiving another fax. The two fax machines need to be compatible. In order to simplify the process of identifying compatibility, fax machines are classified into *groups* with different technical specifications. The two machines need to belong to compatible groups.

The sending machine scans the paper on a line-by-line basis, and transmits the information to the receiving machine, which recreates the document using photocopier technology (for this reason, many fax machines can also operate as photocopiers). Many computers that can be connected to the telephone lines can send faxes directly, without the need to generate a paper copy first: this simplifies the problem of finding the receiving machine busy, as the computer can simply try again later, without human intervention – unfortunately, this also allows unscrupulous advertisers to fax large quantities of *junk fax* mail to unsuspecting recipients.

Minitel

The French telecommunications agency has replaced printed telephone books by an on-line computerised directory enquiries service, called 'Minitel'. Simple terminals with screens are widely available in public places, and personal equipment may be bought or rented. As well as telephone information, a wide variety of commercial and public information is available and theatre and travel tickets can be purchased, as well as more conventional ordering of goods. This is essentially a public *bulletin board* (see above).

Telecommunications

a general term describing the communication of information over a distance. The method of communication is normally via a *cable* (see *wire connector*, page 157) or electro-magnetic radiation. See also *wireless communication*, page 158.

Tele-commuting

is the use of information technology to allow people to work in their own homes, while still being in easy contact with the office. Typically, this involves use of *electronic mail* and *fax* (see above), as well as allowing remote users access to a central computer or network.

Tele-conferencing

including: video-conferencing

is the use of communication links to conduct meetings between people who are geographically separated. The links might be voice-only, or might include pictures, when it is usually referred to as *video-conferencing.*

Videotex

is the overall name given to systems that supply information on television screens. See *Teletext* and *Viewdata,* below, for fuller descriptions.

Teletext

including: Ceefax, Oracle

is a system that uses part of the broadcast television picture unseen to the regular viewer, to supply a variety of information, such as news stories, weather forecasts, train cancellations and so on. With a specially equipped TV set, the viewer can press buttons on a remote control handset to replace the TV picture by simple text pages. Each page is numbered, and all the pages are transmitted in sequence. A particular choice of page is requested by entering the number, after which there is a slight delay until that page is next transmitted; this waiting time limits the number of pages that realistically can be provided. Some pages are linked, and allow the viewer to pass from one page to another more rapidly. All TV channels in the UK offer this service; the BBC version is known as *Ceefax.* The commercial channels were originally known as *Oracle* until the name 'Teletext' was adopted as a brand name. Because the viewer cannot talk back to the provider of the pages of information, this is only a one-way information service.

Viewdata

is the general name given to a *Teletext*-like system (see above) which displays 'pages' of textual information on a television screen, but uses regular phone lines, rather than a broadcast television signal, to transmit information. It is then possible for the user to interact with the system, supplying information, requesting searches of the data, or even ordering goods and services by supplying credit-card information. Because pages are only transmitted after a specific request, very large collections of data can be offered, without penalty to other users.

A5   Databases and Information Retrieval

Although a computer can store enormous amounts of data, this data is useless without appropriate links between individual data items – imagine, for example, what a (printed) telephone directory would be like if it was simply two separate listings of telephone subscribers and their numbers, without the connection that is made by the printed layout between a particular subscriber and their own telephone number! The data is also useless if it cannot be easily retrieved when required — imagine the telephone directory in random rather than alphabetic order!

So too with computerised collections of data. These are generally referred to as **databases** and can vary between a simple name-and-address listing and a massive collection of structured data that provides information to a large business. It is easy to be deceived when one is experimenting with techniques for accessing databases: if a demonstration database can be constructed with tens (rather than millions) of entries, many of the techniques can seem unnecessarily long-winded – if you were certain that your data would never extend to more than 100 entries, it would be sensible to store it in a simple table, as part of your program; when it grew, despite your plans, to 1,000,000 entries no table would be capable of holding it, and it would be necessary to use a disk, and your program would need to use sophisticated methods of disk management.

Because of the need to access this large collection of data in an efficient manner, random access storage devices, such as disks, are essential for a database system.

Large databases usually have many potential users, and so operating system problems of allowing simultaneous use of the same data files arise – the solution to these problems are usually embedded in a complex piece of software, known as the **database management system (DBMS)**.

Not all users will be experienced with computers – often it will be necessary to provide simple **query languages** that allow questions to be asked in something close to English.

Database

sometimes, but infrequently, two words: data base
is a (large) collection of data items and links between them, structured in a way that allows it to be accessed by a number of different applications programs or *query languages* (see below). The term is also used loosely to describe any collection of data.

Data model

including: entity, attribute, entity-relationship diagram, relation

The designers of a large database will normally construct a diagram of the planned database, known as a data model. This will show the things represented in the database (the *entities*) and the information held about them (the *attributes*). For this reason, a data model is sometimes known as an *entity-relationship diagram*. The *relations* between entities will be marked, and from this model the most efficient arrangement of the data will be worked out. Figure A5.1 explains a small portion of a data model.

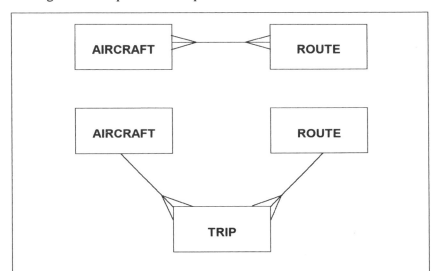

In the top diagram, two entities, **aircraft** and **route,** are identified. Attributes are not shown, but might include the plane number, its type, passenger capacity and so on for the aircraft, and the starting point and destination for the route. There is a relation between these entities: an aircraft can be used on many routes, and a route can be travelled by many aircraft. Such 'many-many' relations are not easy to implement in a database, so the designer breaks this relation, invents a new entity called **trip** which represents one specific journey over that route by one specific aircraft. One aircraft now makes many trips, but each trip is only made by one aircraft. Similarly, one route has many trips over it, but each trip is over just one route. Two such one-many relations are more efficient to implement.

Figure A5.1: *How a data model helps in designing a database*

Database Management System (DBMS)

is the complete collection of software that manages access to, and updating of, a database.

Data dictionary

sometimes known as: data directory

is a file containing descriptions of, and other 'bookkeeping' information about, the data held in a database. It is not usually accessible to users.

Distributed database

is one where several computers on a network each share part of the data and co-operate in making it available to the user.

Flat file

is a database held in a single file – this allows only a very simple structuring of the data, which can only be considered to be on a single level (hence 'flat').

Hierarchical database

is one where the data is held in a *tree* structure (see below) and can be thought of by users as existing on any one of a number of levels.

Information retrieval

or: data retrieval

is the process of extracting meaningful information from stored data; usually the term is used where the collection of stored data is large, typically a database.

Normal form

is a way of structuring the data in a database according to theoretical rules, in order to avoid problems of inefficiency in accessing and maintaining the data.

Query language

is a computer language which allows a database to be interrogated.

Database users without computer expertise might be offered the facility to interrogate a database by accessing a simplified form of query language. The user can ask for information to be extracted, for example, "Which invoices more than 3 months old are recorded in the database that have not yet been paid?" Using words from the query language to link the names of fields, for example date_sent, in the database this general request could become explicit:

SELECT invoices WHERE date_sent < 16-11-94 AND total_owing > 0

Relational database

including: table, view

is one where the data is structured as a series of **tables** and the (relational) database management system provides tools for joining tables together and selecting items from within tables. In this way, each user can be given a different **view** of the data. Relational databases are especially powerful, because the method of storing data in tables makes no assumptions about how the applications programs will access the data, and hence does not restrict the queries in any way.

Schema

including: data description language, subschema

Managing the large amounts of data of different types stored in a modern database requires that descriptions of the data items are held, as well as the data items themselves. This description is usually referred to as the *schema*. The description will be in a **data description language**. The *database management system* (see above) may re-format the data before presenting it to the user, and will make use of individual **subschemas** that describe how that particular user sees the data.

Tree

including: node, branch, root node, parent node, leaf node, terminal node

is a data structure where the data items can be thought of as occurring at different levels. The data items are called **nodes** and the links are called **branches**. The terms **root node, parent node** and **leaf** (or **terminal**) **node** are illustrated in Figure A5.2. Each node must have a link (branch) to the node at the level above.

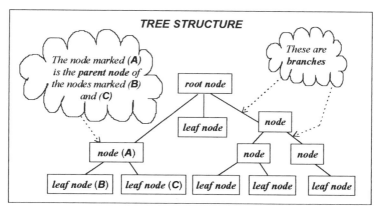

Figure A5.2: A typical tree structure

A6   *Graphics and Design*

Other related terms may be found in section B4 Display Devices.

The display screen of most computer systems uses the same technology as television. Therefore, it is capable of displaying *pictures* as well as text – indeed, text is simply a rather specialised form of picture. Because of this technology, there are many computer applications that use computer power to generate graphics.

Sometimes, the graphics may be an end in themselves, with **painting** or **drawing** packages available to illustrators, to enable them to compose and edit high-quality images. Most computer games are now set in a graphical environment, with exciting animated graphics to underline the action.

Other packages use graphics as part of the design process for books and other printed matter – adding illustrations or decorative borders. In some cases, a photograph (or even 'live-action' video) can be 'retouched' electronically, to add, remove or re-colour some elements of the picture. Many TV graphics are nowadays generated purely electronically.

In other applications, the processing power of the computer is used for calculation, as well as for the pure drawing.

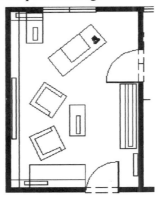

Figure A6.1: *Computer aided architectural design*

Computer aided design packages are used in fields as diverse as architecture and electronics: a builder may design a building on the computer, and call up an itemised list of all the materials to be used in the construction –

the length of pipes, cables, amount of masonry and so on. Or the designer of an electronic printed-circuit board may position the main components to his or her liking, and allow the computer to suggest how the connections should be made, to achieve an efficient design.

Clip art

While computer graphics packages allow the user to draw their own illustrations, many publishers offer computer disks full of professionally-drawn pictures that can be edited to suit an individual user's needs. These are popularly known as 'clip art' because of the way in which they are 'clipped' out of the file and 'pasted' into your own drawing.

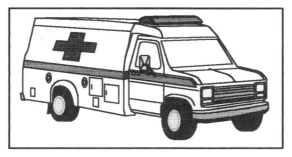

Figure A6.2: *Clip art*

Computer Aided Design (CAD)

including: drafting

This is the use of a computer system to produce drawings or 'blueprints' as part of the design of some construction project; this might be the civil engineering design of a motorway, the layout of components on a printed circuit board, or the drafting of furniture positions in an office or a home — to give just three common examples. This computer aided ***design*** phase is also sometimes known as computer aided ***drafting***. Most modern CAD packages also use the design data as the basis for calculations — for example, of costs, mechanical stresses, quantities needed, etc. With the information available from the design stage, it is possible in many cases for the computer system to control the manufacturing process as well. See also *CAD/CAM*, page 39.

Computer animation

is the creation of apparent movement through the presentation of a sequence of slightly different still pictures. The screen display of a computer is re-drawn every 1/25th of a second, at least, whether it has changed or not, because of the television technology used in display devices. With a fast computer, it is possible to generate a new picture in this time, so that an impression of movement can be created, in the same way as a cinema film creates the illusion of movement from still pictures. Computer animation packages are now routinely used in the television and film industry, particularly where they can mix 'live action' with computer-generated images.

Computer graphics

is the use of the computer to display pictorial information. This can be as simple as a line drawing or chart, or as complicated as an animated sequence of pictures. The output might be shown on the computer screen, printed out as hard copy, or transferred directly to videotape.

Digitiser

also known as: scanner

Many graphics images begin life as drawings on paper and must be converted into a form that a computer graphics package can use. A digitiser scans a drawing and turns it into a *bit map* (see below); this captures the image, but for CAD packages it is necessary to have information about the precise position of important points and lines.

Graphics tablet

also known as: graphics pad
including: stylus, puck

is a device used to input line drawings into a computer. The user draws with a *stylus* on a flat pad or tablet (sometimes called a *graphics pad*), either copying a drawing or working freehand.

Stylus is the name for devices used for drawing on a graphics tablet. The movement of the stylus is detected by the tablet and its software in one of a variety of ways, for example through the use of a wire matrix in the pad or by sensing the angular movement of an arm supporting the stylus. A stylus may be pressure sensitive, producing a darker or more intensely coloured line if pressed firmly.

Puck is a small disk-shaped device, which is moved around on the tablet (or pad) to trace a drawing.

The position of the stylus or puck on the tablet is input to the computer and used to position a cursor on the screen. Subsequent movement causes a drawing on the screen which matches the movements on the tablet. These devices are generally preferred to a mouse for computer drafting packages.

Drawing package

including: line art

Computer graphics packages with the word 'draw' in their titles tend to be of the sort known as *vector graphics* packages, where the instructions for drawing certain basic shapes, such as lines, rectangles, circles and so forth, are stored, rather than the picture itself. These basic shapes, or 'objects', can easily be moved around the drawing, or laid on top of other objects; because of the way they are constructed, they do not interfere with one another, and can be thought of as existing in separate 'layers'; text in drawings would be stored as shapes – each letter a separate object. Because most 'line art' of this sort tends to have only a few elements, there is a considerable advantage in that less storage is needed, as compared to a *painting package* (see below). Scaling the picture up or down in size would not alter the clarity of the drawing. See also *vector graphics*, page 129.

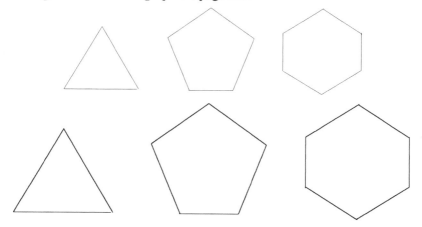

Figure A6.3: Typical output from a drawing package, at two scalings

Painting package

Computer graphics packages with the word 'paint' in their titles tend to be of the sort known as *raster graphics* packages, where a picture is held as a *bit map* (see below) – that is, the state of each individual *pixel* (see page 127) is stored. Text in such a picture would be stored as a bit map. Such drawings use a lot of storage space, because even 'blank' portions of the picture contribute to the size. They can also appear jagged when scaled up or down in size. However, for freehand drawings, and areas of tone, such packages are better than *drawing packages* (see above). See also *raster graphics,* page 128.

Figure A6.4: *Typical output from a painting package*

Bit map

is the use of groups of bits to hold the settings of individual *pixels* (see page 127) of a picture. Each pixel is allocated a group of bits to define its characteristics, for example colour. Individual pixels can be changed by altering the appropriate bits in the bit map. Graphic images prepared in a 'painting' package are usually held as a bit map, but images produced by a 'drawing' package are usually held as individual objects. See *drawing package* and *painting package* above. See also *vector graphics* page 129.

A7   *Modelling and Simulation*

Imagine having to design and build a new bypass to divert traffic round a town. Before starting on such a venture it would be wise to check on the cost and compare that with the advantages to be gained. Although it is quite possible to produce accurate costings, it is harder to work out how wide the bypass should be (should it be dual or single carriageway, for example) or what route it should take to reduce the traffic flow through the town. By the time the road is built the money will have been spent and the bypass may not be effective. When data on current traffic flow has been collected and likely future traffic requirements have been assessed a model can be produced. **Modelling** attempts to show what is happening now and the results of the intended alterations. The model produced is a mathematical description of the rate of traffic flow at all points of interest. The details of this model can be changed, for example by increasing the expected amount of traffic, to see whether this causes any problems. Once the model has been tested with these conditions it can then be judged how good the proposed changes would be. The bypass could then be built, with the likelihood that it would be worthwhile, or it could be abandoned, as not useful enough, having only had the cost of the exploration.

It is when you want to test and use a mathematical model that a computer would be used. The computer can quickly carry out the necessary calculations (many of which are repeated but quite simple) and show the results using tables of numbers or diagrams. **Simulation** is the running of the design.

Weather forecasting uses a computer simulation. Data is gathered from many sources at different times and from this the computer predicts what weather we are likely to expect in the near or far future. From experience we know that accuracy can vary from being very good to being dramatically wrong. The prediction can only be as good as the model. Economic forecasting is also performed in a similar way, but often lacks the accuracy of even a weather forecast.

Any model is limited by human understanding and the need for it to be sufficiently simple to allow results to be calculated in a reasonable time.

Computer simulations are also used in training. A flight simulator is used to prepare pilots to cope with anything from standard flying and landing, to dealing with emergencies without putting anyone's life at risk. A flight simulator can range from a simple screen display to a full-size mock-up of the flight cabin with movement effects.

In education, computer simulation can be used to show a process that would normally be impossible to demonstrate because it would be too dangerous, too expensive or would take too long. In a simulation dealing with a nuclear reactor station, alterations could be made that would not be allowed at a visit to such a station! Similarly, in the field of genetics, alterations could be simulated on a reasonable timescale rather than waiting months or years for even simple processes to be checked.

In silicon chip design, a simulation is used to show how the circuitry would behave. The design is adjusted until the required response is achieved. This saves the expense and time of producing, testing and having to change a series of prototypes. In these circumstances **emulation** software could be used to check computer behaviour for various programs before the new chip becomes available.

Model

A model is a sequence of ideas that attempt to represent a process realistically. At some stage these ideas are expressed mathematically as a set (or collection) of equations. The accuracy of this model is limited by the knowledge of the process being modelled, the time available to produce the model, the availability of input data and how quickly results are required.

Modelling

is the construction of a *model* (see above) by mathematical analysis and the testing of proposed models in known situations.

Simulation

is the use of a computer program to predict the likely behaviour of a real-life system. A mathematical *model* (see above) of the system is constructed in a form that can be run on a computer. This may require special programs to be written or may be achieved using existing packages, for example making financial predictions using spreadsheets.

Emulation

is a very precise form of *simulation* (see above) which should mimic exactly the behaviour of the circumstances that it is simulating.

An *emulator* (see below) may enable one type of computer to operate as if it were a different type of computer.

Emulation may be used by printers to enable them to behave like a different printer. This may enable them to be used with a wide variety of computer software.

Emulator

is a program that allows a computer to behave as if it were a different type of computer. An emulator enables:

- software to be developed which will run on computers not yet built
- software to be used on a type of computer other than the type it was designed for
- software to be tested when it would otherwise use expensive resources
- a computer to be used as a peripheral, appearing to the host computer to have the characteristics expected. This enables microcomputers to act as terminals to larger computer systems.

An emulator is often much slower than the host computer because of the extra processing involved.

A8   Virtual Reality

Virtual reality systems transport the user into an environment created by the computer. Computer-controlled graphics are used to generate realistic scenes with which the user can interact.

To provide realism and to prevent distraction from the immediate environment, the user may wear a headset. The headset incorporates earphones to play the appropriate soundtrack directly into the ears, while small video screens, in goggles covering the eyes, ensure that the only images seen are those generated by the computer.

When the head moves, the simulation changes the image in response to where the user is now 'looking'. This gives the illusion of moving through the scene. The use of the headset provides a powerful psychological effect, giving a strong feeling of realism. An alternative to using a headset is the use of wrap-around displays with stereo sound for group participation.

To increase further the feeling of experiencing the simulated environment, a *data glove* can be worn. This is an input device that enables the position of the fingers and the orientation of the hand to be sensed by the computer. It provides the opportunity for the user to point at or 'touch' objects, which will produce some response from the system.

Full virtual reality is a technology that is still in its infancy; it is very demanding in its requirements for resources. It needs high-quality three-dimensional graphics. The need for immediate and smooth change of scene requires fast processing. There are also enormous storage requirements. However by using **CD-ROM** and accepting lower standards of visual presentation on a screen, low-quality virtual reality can be produced to run on relatively modest computer systems; these products are being sold as virtual reality.

Data glove

is an input device worn on the hand of a user of a virtual reality system. Typically, it enables the position of the fingers and the orientation of the hand to be sensed by the system. In most systems, when the user 'touches' a simulated object, there is no physical sensation returned to the hand. Greater realism is possible in systems which do provide this kind of feedback.

Headset

is an input and output device, like a helmet, worn by a user of a virtual reality
system. It gives the wearer the impression of being within the computer-
generated scene, with sound provided through headphones and vision through
small video screens in goggles worn over the eyes. The headset senses changes
of position of the head and inputs this to the computer so that the simulation
can be changed appropriately. Since the user is isolated from sounds and
visions, other than those provided by the virtual reality system, there is a very
strong sense of being within the simulated environment.

Virtual reality system

also known as: VR system

is a computer system that provides a simulated environment by three-
dimensional graphical images and an appropriate soundtrack. It gives the user
the impression of being within the environment. The graphical images are
often of rather poor quality but these are expected to become more realistic as
advances in the technology are made.

A9   *Control*

Other terms related to the use of computers in controlling processes and devices will be found in B7 Communications Devices and Control Devices.

The use of computers to make machines do what we want them to - called **control** - grew out of the extensive use of mechanical devices and electromagnetic switches (relays). In telephone exchanges, traffic lights and lifts, control used to be achieved by the use of mechanically operated switching systems. Other methods were designed to control the operation of machines, made up of devices which reacted to conditions in the environment such as temperature, pressure, speed, position. Large manufacturing plants were built controlled by these methods.

The development of microprocessors and microcomputers made it possible to improve the reliability of existing systems and to make them more flexible. In a modern airliner the computer system is capable of controlling take-off and landing as well as automatically maintaining course, speed and altitude. The computers used in cars take over part of the control of the car engine from the driver. The operation of washing machines and video equipment is frequently managed by microprocessors.

Control may be exercised remotely, in which case control signals are sent from the controller to the device. These signals may be transmitted in any of the ways which are used to pass data for example through wires, or as radio or infra-red signals.

Control systems may be either passive or re-active. In a **passive system** the controlled device, once it has been set going, will perform a predetermined set of activities regardless of the circumstances. A **re-active system** will vary its behaviour in response to different situations. By using programmable chips, connected to suitable sensors, it is now common for systems to respond to the information provided by these sensors. Combining control and observation, through the use of sensors, has made it possible to extend the scope of automatic **process control**, for example in the manufacture and packaging of chemical products.

Automation
is the use of machines or systems to perform tasks as an alternative to using people.

CAD/CAM

including: computer assisted manufacturing (CAM)

is the use of the output from a computer aided design (CAD) process as input to control a *computer assisted manufacturing (CAM)* process. This can be an integrated process in which the manufacturing happens automatically and is important in the development of new products. See *computer aided design,* page 29.

Data capture

including: sampling, data logging

is the *sampling* (collection at specified intervals) of output from external sensors. This data may be used to control a process. *Data logging* is the capture and storage of data for later use, thus data captured in a control process may be logged for later analysis of the process.

Feedback

including: closed loop feedback, open loop feedback

is the use of data from sensors as input to the controlling program. In this way the result of previous actions becomes input which contributes to selecting the next action. If the response to the feedback is automatic (there is no human operator involvement), the process is called *closed loop*; if an operator is involved, it is called *open loop*. In most situations where feedback is used to control position, for example stacking boxes on shelves, the correct position is achieved by an iterative process, in which a move is followed by a position check, each move bringing it closer to the required position, until the correct position is reached.

Fly by wire

is a method of controlling an aeroplane in flight. The flaps, rudder and other control surfaces of the aeroplane are operated by motors. These motors are controlled by (electrical) signals which are created as a result of actions by the pilot. This kind of flight control system involves the use of computers to analyse the pilot's intentions and thus work out the right amount of movement of the control surfaces; the computers can over-ride the pilot in situations which would endanger the aeroplane.

G-code

is a form of computer language used by the control systems of some machine tools.

Numeric control

also called: computer numeric control (CNC)

generally refers to the automatic control of machines such as lathes and milling machines. Some numerically controlled machines simply obey a preset program of instructions, while more advanced machines can react to *feedback* (see above) from *sensors* (see page 161).

Paper tape

including: paper tape punch, paper tape reader

is sometimes still used as the means of program and data input to machine tools. A pattern of holes punched in the tape is used to represent the data. In order to prepare the tape a *paper tape punch* is attached to the computer on which the program and data are prepared while a *tape reader* is used as an input device to the machine tool.

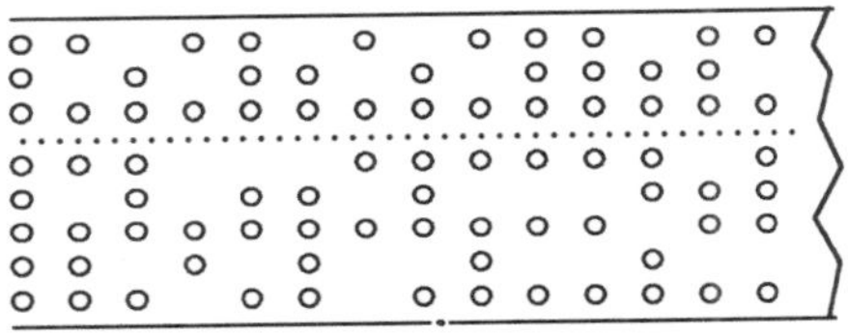

Figure A9.1: Punched paper tape

Process control

including: integrated manufacturing

is the automatic monitoring and control of an industrial activity by a computer that is programmed to respond to the *feedback* (see above) signals from *sensors* (see page 161). The operation controlled may be as small as a single machine packing boxes or as extensive as the control of an automated bakery, where the mixing, cooking and packaging are controlled within a single *integrated manufacturing* process.

Robot

including: robot arm

is a computer-controlled mechanical device which is sufficiently flexible to be able to do a variety of tasks. Robots are frequently used to do jobs where consistent performance is required (such as paint spraying motor cars) or where there is some danger to humans performing the task (such as the handling of toxic materials). A *robot arm* is a relatively simple fixed robot capable of picking things up, positioning them, etc.

Telemetry

is the use of communications (usually radio) and measuring sensors to achieve control of machines and instruments at a distance. For example, the control of satellites and space probes, or the monitoring and control of the performance of formula 1 racing cars, where the technicians can adjust the engine control system on the car from the pits while the race is in progress.

A10 Numerical and Scientific Computing

The first computers were seen simply as calculating devices, able to carry out lengthy and tedious mathematical calculations without error and at high speed. They made existing trigonometric and logarithm tables unnecessary, as computers were able to calculate values when needed, as fast as they could look up stored values – although at that stage, the individual scientist did not conceive of a personal computer, and continued to work with portable calculating devices such as slide rules and tables.

The focus of computing has now shifted away from the purely numerical, but nevertheless there are still major uses for mathematical programming. The statistical analysis of large amounts of data involves considerable amounts of computation, as well as the ordering and sorting of the data.

Another area involving numerical computing is the deciphering of codes – **cryptanalysis**. Strictly, a *code* is any scheme for substituting one representation of data for another, as in *character code*. The correct term for a coded message, where the intention is to conceal information, is a **cipher**.

The process of enciphering messages – **cryptography** – also involves numeric computing because it is usual to turn textual messages into numbers (A=01, B=02, CAT=030120 etc.) and to perform mathematical operations on the resulting large numbers, in order to turn them into a cipher.

Some of the techniques encountered in numerical uses of computing belong to the mathematical branch known as **numerical analysis**. Some of these techniques are defined below. In calculating the values that appear in mathematical tables, the computer often uses power series; sometimes a calculation is done in an indirect way, using **iteration**, where a 'trial' answer is repeatedly refined, until it is approximately correct.

Algorithm
is a specific procedure for a computer that will either accomplish some task or solve a problem. An algorithm is roughly equivalent to a computer program. Algorithms may be described in any suitable form. These include instructions in words, (such as, Figure A10.1, below), instructions in a computer language or diagrams. Methods of writing or describing algorithms form an important part of computer science and are beyond the scope of this glossary.

Loop
is a group of instructions which is repeatedly executed. For example, to produce payslips for several workers, the instructions for one payslip are

repeated many times with different data.

The instructions in a loop may be repeated a fixed number of times or an unspecified number of times, with the instructions being repeated until some condition is satisfied.

The use of loops is common in mathematical and computing processes. For an example of the use of a loop see *iteration (mathematical)*, below.

Combinatorics
including: enumeration

is the branch of mathematics to do with counting or *enumerating*. In using computer systems to search for alternative routes through a road network, for example, it will be important to ensure that all possible combinations are considered, and that extra work is not done by considering routes that have already been looked at. Combinatorial *algorithms* (see above) are designed to take care of details such as this.

Cryptanalysis
including: cipher, cipher breaking

is the *'breaking'* of *ciphers*. Nowadays, this is almost always done by computer. Captured cipher messages are analysed to see if patterns emerge that will indicate the method of coding, after which further analysis may indicate the precise *key* (see *cryptography*, below) used in the enciphering.

Cryptography
including: cipher, secret messages, key

is the science of sending *secret messages*, or *ciphers*. In communicating by code, it is usual for everyone to use the same method, but to have some personal (and secret) *key* that modifies the method in a way that makes the message remain secure, even if the method is known. Generally, textual messages are converted into numbers before being enciphered, resulting in a very large number of perhaps a hundred or so digits. The method is an *algorithm* (see above) that processes that number but uses the key number as a vital part of the calculation. See *public key cryptography* below.

Data Encryption Standard (DES)

is a standard method of encrypting data, developed by the US government. The method specifies how a *key* (see *cryptography*, above) is used to encode the message in a standard way. It is believed that the method alone is secure enough, without knowledge of the key, for it to be published. Making the method publicly available means that computer manufacturers can develop software and hardware for easy implementation of the method.

Iteration (mathematical)

is a mathematical procedure for solving equations, where an initial estimate is made of the answer, and the result of using this (possibly quite poor) guess is used to improve the answer. If this process is repeated, or re-iterated, enough times, the desired answer can be found to any degree of accuracy. See Figure A10.1 for an example of iteration. See also *loop*, above.

CALCULATING A SQUARE ROOT

We know that the square root of 2 is 1.414214 to 6 decimal places. An iterative method of calculating this is to take a guess (even a very bad guess) such as 3. If this first guess is then used as x in the calculation:

$$y = \frac{1}{2}\left[x + \frac{2}{x} \right]$$

*you get an answer y=1.833, which is **closer** to the known answer than the original guess. The value of this method is that if you then repeat the calculation, using 1.833 as the guess, the next **iterate** is closer still, 1.46212. In fact, after only two further iterations, the method is giving the known answer correct to six decimal places. Finding the formulas that 'work' in these situations is part of **numerical analysis**.*

Figure A10.1: *An example of iteration*

Public key cryptography

including: one-way functions, trapdoor functions, RSA algorithm
Some mathematical operations are easy to do, but in practice impossible to undo. As a simple example, it is easy to multiply together 11 and 13 to get 143, but it takes an amount of trial-and-error to work back from 143 to the (only) factors 11 and 13. If the numbers involved had hundreds or thousands of digits, rather than just two, the amount of trial and error involved would mean that even a fast computer might be unable to find the factors in an acceptably short time. Such operations – easy to do, and impossible to undo in a realistic time – are known as *one-way functions*. If the operation is one like the multiplication above, where some secret knowledge (like the numbers 11 and 13) provides a short-cut, they are known as *trapdoor functions*. These can be used as the basis for a simple but secure coding system, as shown in Figure A10.2. The best-known such function was developed by the

mathematicians Rivest, Shamir and Adleman, and is, unsurprisingly, called the *RSA algorithm*.

	A public directory is published – for everyone in the code system, it tells the whole world what **key** is used to send messages to that person. This is a (big) number that can be used to encode messages. The *de*coding part is secret: only one person knows that!
	I want to send a message to you. I write my message out, substituting A=01, B=02 etc. and get a (long) number which represents my message.
	Now I look up your key in the public directory and use it to turn my message into another long number – this is done in a way that no-one except you can decode – even *I* can't, unless I look back at my original message.
	You receive my message, and using your very secret decoding method, turn it back into the original message.
	How do you know that the message was *really* from me? Anyone could look up your key in the public directory and send a misleading message that claimed to be from me! I can *prove* it was from me, like this:
	With my message, I include my name and address, but before I code this, I use my own secret de-coding key to turn the name and address part into a scrambled version.
	Now I code the whole message – the message itself *and* the previously scrambled name and address.
	You receive this two-part message, and use *your* secret de-coder to extract the plain message and the scrambled name and address. You read the message, and need to check that it is from me.
	You take the scrambled part, look me up in the directory and see what my public coding key is. Using this will unscramble the name and address, and you are confident that it *was* from me, because I am the only person in the world who knows what my *de*-coding key is.

Figure A10.2: *How a public-key cryptosystem works*

Monte Carlo method

A whimsical name which comes from the use of chance (usually *random numbers* – see below – rather than roulette wheels) in simulation. In exploring the behaviour of a complex system (which might be chemical, physical, biological, human, etc.), the overall behaviour of the system may be too complicated to specify confidently in mathematical terms. If the many small decisions in the system *can* be easily specified, then the behaviour of the system can be simulated, using random numbers to model a large number of small decisions. For example, migration of people between towns in the UK might be too complicated to specify mathematically, but information *is* available on how many people move from London to Edinburgh (say) each year. The overall behaviour of the population can be explored by selecting one resident of London, and generating a random number to see if that individual will stay or move, and if so, where to. By repeating this for the whole population of the UK, predictions about future population trends will be possible, even if the mathematics is not fully understood.

Numerical analysis

is the branch of mathematics that studies the methods (such as *power series, iteration, recursion*) mentioned in this section. Numerical analysts are interested in methods of computing, but are not necessarily heavy users of computers in practice.

Power series

Some mathematical quantities (like π) can be computed using a series such as:

$$\pi = 4\left(\frac{1}{2} + \frac{1}{3} - \frac{1}{2^3.3} - \frac{1}{3^3.3} + \frac{1}{2^5.5} + \frac{1}{3^5.5} - \cdots\right)$$

Depending on how accurate an answer is needed, more or less of the terms being added together can be included. If you stop computing the series above after four terms, the answer 3.117284 is accurate to (only) 1 decimal place — if more are needed, adding in (say) four more terms increases the accuracy to 3 decimal places. *Numerical analysis* (see above) is the branch of mathematics that is used to design suitable power series.

Recursion

is a mathematical way of defining a computation in terms of a reduced version of itself. This may seem like a paradox, but because this method is close to the way some mathematical operations are programmed in a computer, it can be very efficient. See Figure A10.3 for two examples.

USING RECURSION

Factorials

The factorial of a number, written as 7!, 3! and so on, is defined as:

    7! = 7 × 6 × 5 × 4 × 3 × 2 × 1

    3! = 3 × 2 × 1   *and so on.*

*Factorials often turn up in **combinatorial algorithms**. Another way of defining a factorial is to say that:*

    7! = 7 × 6!

    3! = 3 × 2!   *or, in general, n! = n × (n-1)!*

*Thus, each factorial is defined in terms of a smaller factorial. This is a **recursive** definition. To make this work, it is necessary to give the smallest factorial 1! a specific value (in this case 1 itself).*

Sorting

*A list (of numbers, or words — anything) often has to be sorted into order (numerical or alphabetic, say). One way of defining the process **recursively**, in a way that can be easy to program, is as follows:*

      Find the earliest item in the list;

      print that out, and remove it from the list;

             now repeat the whole process, but using the new,

                 shorter, list.

In a similar way to the factorial example above, it is necessary to program the computer to stop taking items off the list when you have shortened it so far that there is nothing left!

Figure A10.3: *Two examples of recursion*

Prime numbers

are numbers like 7, 19, 23 and so on, which have no factors other than themselves and one – that is, they cannot be made by multiplying other numbers together (as 24 can be made by multiplying 6 × 4, or 3 × 8, and so on). Prime numbers are important in computing because they form the basis of ciphers (see *cryptography*, above), and also because searching for new prime numbers is a good test of mathematical programming techniques. Other uses of prime numbers are in the design of algorithms for *hashing* (see page 6), and (pseudo) *random number generation*, see below.

Random number generation

including: pseudo-random number generator

Many *simulations* (see page 34) on a computer need to make use of random numbers, in a similar way to 'tossing a coin' in order to make a decision. Most programming languages include a random number function, that gives the user a suitable number, as if it had been chosen at random — numbers between 1 and 6, for example, to simulate the throw of dice in a game. Because computer programs cannot be truly random, a ***pseudo-random number generator*** is used, which gives numbers with the appearance of being random. See *Monte Carlo method,* above, for more information.

Numeric display format

also known as: display format

is the way in which numbers are printed on documents or shown on a screen. Most software, typically spreadsheets, will require the user to indicate how numbers are to be displayed or printed. For example, the result of the calculation 4892/75 is 65.22666666666... , but displaying all these digits is not really sensible (or may not be possible).

The software asks the user to set ***display formats***. These often use the hash symbol, #, to represent digits. Thus #.### means a number rounded to three decimal places. A zero, 0, may also be used to display leading or trailing zeros, otherwise these would not be displayed. Other examples from a typical spreadsheet are shown in Figure A10.4.

DISPLAY FORMATS

#.####   Numbers will be displayed rounded to 4 decimal places
thus 65.22666666666 will be displayed as   65.2267

#.00   Numbers will be displayed rounded to 2 decimal places
with trailing zeros if necessary
thus 230 will be displayed as   230.00
and 34.3 will be displayed as   34.30

0   numbers will be displayed as integers (whole numbers)
rounded to the nearest whole number
thus 237.41 will be displayed as   237
and 34.8 will be displayed as   35

These examples have all been presented with the decimal points aligned.

Figure A10.4: *Formats for displaying numbers*

A11   Sound

This section is concerned with the use of computers to generate, store, communicate and manipulate sound.

Most of the terms used when working with computer-generated sound belong to the terminology of music or sound. There are however some terms whose use in a computing context need to be defined.

Electronic reproduction of natural sound has been available for many decades. The ability to generate natural sounds electronically – **sound synthesis** – was developed long before computers. Sound is produced by the continuous vibration of air. This means that it has analog properties. A microphone converts sound energy (air vibrations) into electrical energy (fluctuating voltage and current). In the opposite process a loudspeaker converts electrical energy into sound. These are both analog devices, since they create or use varying electrical energy. The earliest forms of sound synthesis worked by creating and manipulating varying electrical currents, they worked entirely on analog principles. With the use of digital computer techniques the more recent digital audio systems have been developed. These systems use digital methods to create, process and store sounds but receive analog input from microphones and produce analog output for loudspeakers.

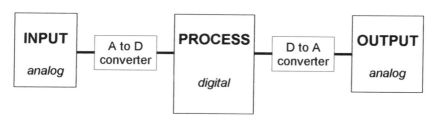

Figure A11.1: *A sound system*

The electrical output from microphones is analog (that is, it consists of a continuously fluctuating voltage). It has to be converted into a digital form if it is to be stored on a digital device (for example, a compact disk) or if it is to be transmitted or manipulated in a digital form. Loudspeakers or headphones require analog signals. The conversion of analog (sound) signals to digital is achieved by a sampling process while the conversion of digital to analog is achieved by adding the values of the bits in the digital representation.

Both analog and digital methods are used to transmit, record, manipulate and create sounds. Digital methods involve the use of computers (or microprocessors) to manipulate data. Thus many pieces of digital musical or sound equipment will contain microprocessors.

The use of computers to create sounds involve sound or speech synthesis. Many microcomputers have (or can be fitted with) appropriate chips so that they can output speech; for example the computer can 'speak' words as well as display them on the screen. The use of voice input is being developed, but there are difficulties yet to be overcome before it can be the normal method of communication between people and computers. As far as the computer is concerned sound is just another form of data which it can create, store, manipulate or output, provided the right input and output devices are available and connected. The manipulation of sound data may be done by software or by hardware within the computer or attached to the computer.

Sound synthesis

also known as: sound generation

including: analog and digital sound generation, subtractive synthesis, Frequency Modulation (FM), Phase Distortion (PD), Linear Arithmetic (LA), additive synthesis

is the use of electronic devices for creating sounds, sometimes called *sound generation*. The sounds may be generated using either analog or digital techniques. Electronically generated sound can create notes which are like those produced by a variety of musical instruments.

Analog sound generation has been used for a very long time (well over 50 years). Usually, the sound is produced by starting with a complex waveform, containing many harmonics, which is produced by an oscillator. Electronic filter circuits are then used to modify the sound by removing some of these harmonics. This process is called *subtractive synthesis*.

Digital sound generation is a recent development in which numbers representing sound waves are manipulated. A variety of methods are used to create the sounds, some of them unique to a particular manufacturer. The most commonly used synthesis methods are:

Frequency Modulation (FM) in which the digital representation of a number of pure waveforms are combined with each other to create a complex compound sound.

Phase Distortion (PD) in which the digital representation of a waveform is
modified, by speeding up the rate at which the wave is generated, to
produce a complex waveform. This complex waveform is then modified
as in an analog synthesiser.

Linear Arithmetic (LA) in which sampled sounds are used as well as pure
tones as the start of the process. Arithmetic operations are then carried
out on the values of the bit patterns representing the sounds. (See *sound
sampler*, below.)

Additive synthesis is a computer software method in which the user selects a
mixture of harmonics and the computer calculates the values for the
waveform at very small successive time intervals. In all cases the digital
values for the sound are turned into sound signals by a digital-to-analog
converter. Different methods of creating sounds produce different
qualities of sound.

Music synthesiser

*including: synthesiser, analog synthesiser, digital synthesiser, multi-timbral
synthesiser, polyphony*

is an electronic device for creating sounds. It is often called just a *synthesiser*.
The sounds may be generated electronically using either analog or digital
techniques (see *sound generator*, below). Most synthesisers have a piano-
style keyboard and need to be connected to an amplifier with loudspeakers for
the sounds they produce to be heard.

Analog synthesisers are usually intended to be used as musical instruments
to be played, and most do not have the ability to store the sounds they
create.

Digital synthesisers generally incorporate some form of digital storage and
frequently have a built-in store of ready-made sounds. Digital
synthesisers generally offer a much greater variety of sounds and a wider
range of manipulation options than analog synthesisers. For example, a
multi-timbral synthesiser can play two or more different sounds at the
same time, or produce a number of different notes at the same time
(*polyphony*), or a combination of both of these capabilities in the same
synthesiser.

Envelope

including: ADSR (attack, decay, sustain, release)

is a shape which is used to describe the changes in volume (amplitude), pitch (frequency) and timbre (quality) of a note as it changes with time. The form of sound envelopes are normally used in *sound synthesis* (see above). One commonly used way of describing a volume envelope is known as *ADSR*, an acronym for Attack, Decay, Sustain and Release.

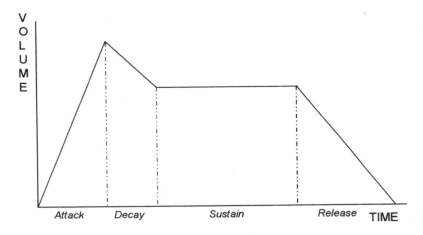

Figure A11.2: Volume envelope

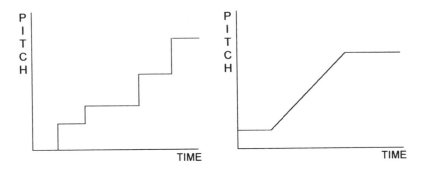

Figure A11.3: Two pitch envelopes

Attack is the rate at which an envelope rises to its initial peak before starting to decay. For example percussive sounds (piano or drums) have a high attack rate for their volume (amplitude). *Decay* is the rate at which an envelope falls from its initial peak to a steady (sustain) level. *Sustain* is the level at which an envelope remains whilst a key is still pressed after the initial attack and decay stages. *Release* is the rate at which an envelope fades away from its sustain level when the key is released.

MIDI (Musical Instrument Digital Interface)

including: MIDI channel, MIDI standard, MIDI code.

A musical instrument digital interface, MIDI (frequently, but incorrectly, referred to as a MIDI interface) is a particular form of *serial interface* (see page 154) built into or added to the parts of an electronic music system. The interface allows electronic music data to be passed in both directions between parts of the system. The links between parts of the system are called *MIDI channels*.

The form of the interface and the structure of the data are defined by the *MIDI standard*, which was agreed between the major manufacturers of electronic musical instruments in 1983. The standard defines the codes (*MIDI codes*) to be used for musical data, for example the pitch of a note and its volume. These codes allow music data to be passed between devices from different manufacturers in the same way that *ASCII* codes (see *character set*, page 178) allow alphanumeric data to be passed between different computers.

Music keyboard

including: keyboard

Any electronic music device which is controlled by a keyboard similar to a piano is called a music keyboard or a *keyboard*. The keys, which are arranged like the black and white keys on a piano, are frequently supplemented by switches, sliders or other ways of setting and changing the electronic signals produced by or used by the device.

Sound controller

including: musical instrument controller, audio controller

is a hardware device which controls sounds generated by a sound source.
Controllers usually do not produce sounds themselves, though they may be
made to look like (and be used like) a musical instrument, for example a piano
keyboard or a guitar. These are called *musical instrument controllers*. Some
controllers use joysticks, sliders or wheels. These may be built into other
controllers or attached to a musical instrument. Control of sounds is usually
achieved by using *MIDI codes* (see *MIDI*, above). There are also *audio
controllers*, which can generate (MIDI) control signals from audio sounds.
With an audio controller looking like a microphone, a user can sing into it
while 'playing' a synthesised sound from a connected sound generator, and
thus control the sound produced.

Sound generator

also known as: sound source

is a digital device capable of producing sounds as part of an electronic music
system; it is sometimes called a *sound source*. A range of such devices exist,
which create sounds similar to those produced by particular musical
instruments, such as drum machines, electric guitars or electronic organs.
Music synthesisers (see above) are an example of a sound generator with a
piano-type keyboard which is used to play them, but most sound generators
have no direct means of being played as if they were musical instruments.
Some have a collection of pre-defined sounds and some have synthesising
capability. If the sounds can be altered then there will be controls to do so.
The sounds may be accessed via MIDI, to be used as input to a sequencer or a
music controller, or the device may be attached to a computer as a dedicated
peripheral.

Sound sampler

including: sampling rate, sampling resolution

is an example of a *digital sampler* (see page 161), in which the device receives
sound signals from a microphone (or other sound source) and analyses them.
It makes and stores the digital measurements from this analysis. By
performing this process of analysis, measurement and storage very quickly and
very frequently, the sampler converts the signal into a digital representation of
the sound.

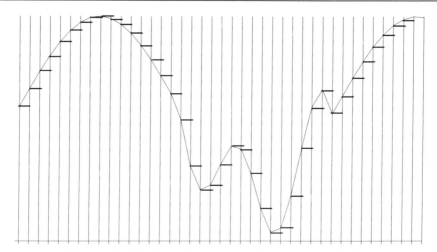

Figure A11.4: *A continuous waveform with sample levels*

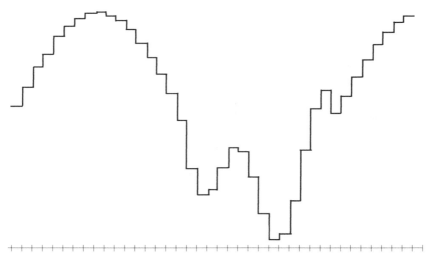

Figure A11.5: *The sampled waveform from Figure A11.4*

The succession of values from this sampling can be processed, stored or fed through a digital-to-analog converter to reproduce the sound. Sound sampling is the standard method of capturing sound for storage or manipulation in digital form.

The quality of sound produced using a sound sampler depends upon the *sampling rate* and the *sampling resolution*.

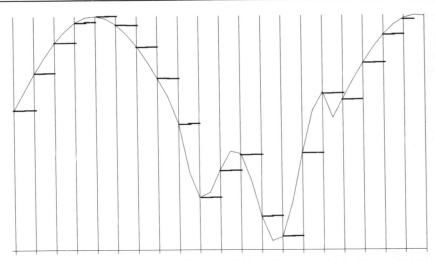

Figure A11.6: *The same waveform, sampling frequency halved - resulting in much cruder sound quality*

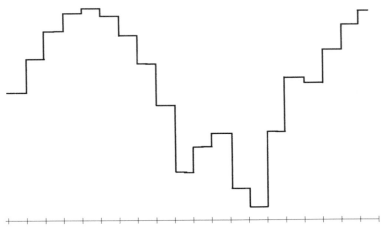

Figure A11.7: *The sampled waveform from Figure A11.6*

Sampling rate is the frequency at which samples are taken and is usually twice the maximum frequency of the sound being sampled.

Sampling resolution is the number of bits used for data storage, which is 16 bits for CD players but may be only 8 bits in some personal computers.

Sound mixer

including: channel, music channel

is an operator-controlled electronic device for combining sound signals. The operator selects how input signals are to be combined to form one or more output signals. The paths or connections for input and output signals are known as *channels* or *music channels*.

Sound processor

is the general term for electronic sound equipment which can take a sound signal as input, modify the signal and output the new signal. The processing may use either analog or digital techniques, but the use of digital methods is now more common. Most sound processors have a particular function, for example echo units, reverberation units, graphic equalisers, noise reduction units. All of these work in *real-time* (see *sequencer*, below).

Sound processing software on a suitable computer can do the same things that individual sound processing items achieve. Thus a computer may be used as a general-purpose sound processor.

Computer-based music system

including: digital sound system

is an arrangement of electronic music devices and a computer linked together so that music and other sounds, such as speech and singing, can be captured, stored, manipulated, generated or reproduced. These systems will probably contain both digital and analog components. Where only digital processing components are used it is referred to as a *digital sound system*.

Music work station

is a collection of connected music-generating and sound-manipulating equipment. A typical arrangement will include a keyboard, a synthesiser and a sequencer. They are increasingly likely to include a computer with appropriate software. See *computer-based music system*, above.

Sequencer

including: real-time entry, step-time entry

is a digital device which can store a set of representations of notes, rhythms
and other musical data for replaying at a later time. It may also include
facilities for editing or for producing repeated patterns. Sequencers may range
from the very simple, capable of storing only a small number of notes or a
single chord, to the complex, capable of simultaneously handling many
independent musical parts. Sequencers are often built into *synthesisers* (see
music synthesiser, above) and drum machines or other electronic music
devices. One example of the use of a sequencer is to play a piece of stored
music at different speeds without the distortion of pitch, which happens if the
speed of a tape recorder is varied. Another is to change the sound of a series
of notes previously entered, rather like changing the colours of parts of a
computer-generated picture with an art program.

Music parts can be entered into a sequencer in one of two ways, *real-time* or
step-time.

Real-time entry has the musical information provided by playing the notes
with the correct relative time intervals. They need not be the actual
intervals since the sequencer can modify the speed (tempo).

Step-time entry has the time interval between each note defined by the person
entering the musical information.

SMPTE codes

SMPTE is an acronym for the Society of Motion Picture and TV Engineers
(USA). The codes are an agreed set of standards which make it possible to
synchronise sound and video signals.

Speech recognition

including: voice print

is a process of analysing a spoken word and comparing it with those known to
the computer system. The use of *voice prints* (like finger prints, each person's
voice is unique) for security purposes is increasing. It is already possible to
use voice input to computers. However, the differences between the same
words spoken by different people still make this an unreliable process requiring
substantial memory and processing power.

Speech synthesis

including: speech synthesiser, phoneme

is the production of sounds resembling human speech by electronic methods.
This is achieved either by the use of computer software or through hardware, a
speech synthesiser. A speech synthesiser is a piece of hardware, usually built
into a computer. It is an output device that generates sound in response to
input data, usually in the form of alphanumeric characters. The sound is
produced either by selecting an appropriate sound from a collection of stored
sounds or by breaking down the input data into its individual speech
components, called *phonemes*, for example the vowel sound in 'meet' or
'meat', which are output in sequence.

A12   Hypermedia Systems

Hypermedia systems are interactive computer systems which are concerned principally with the storage of data (and its associated information retrieval) for reference purposes. They are usually organised so that the user can obtain information in a number of ways. Often called **hypertext** systems, they store text in such a way that users are able to construct their own links between different parts of the text. The multi-level approach to text acquisition, storage, analysis, comparison, retrieval and editing includes a comprehensive command structure which allows users to move through a document. This may be achieved by the use of pre-programmed links, through techniques such as *browsing*, or by searching for specific words. The system will remember the path taken.

Hypermedia is an extension of hypertext and also includes related graphics (still, animated and moving video) and sound.

The data is held in a non-linear structure using nodes and, for each node, a small number of links (typically 2, 3 or 4) are available to related nodes. Using on-screen menus, often presented on a menu-bar, it is possible to move through the system in a variety of search patterns. Starting with a main index, the user can choose a path which introduces the context of a particular subject and then, having noticed some point of special interest, can change the search pattern to follow the context of that new subject. The system might also allow the user to search for associated themes by using key words in the particular screen being displayed at that time.

The change in the type of information generated by calls into such a system can be dramatic. For example, in a system which was apparently associated with an art gallery, the user might choose to look at information about one particular artist which could include a screen display of that artist's pictures. Then, seeing a subject of interest depicted in one of the paintings, choose to look at paintings by other artists on the same subject. If the subject happened to be people playing musical instruments, the next step might be to choose to hear some music associated with those instruments. This might then lead to a topic dealing with the production of sound, and then to information about the physics of wave motion.

The usefulness of such a system is dependent on the type of data structure which it employs, the size of the database and the access time. The ease of use might be related to the physical process of using the menus, where a touch-screen might have considerable advantages over a mouse or the arrow keys.

Multimedia

is the presentation of information by a computer system using graphics, animation, sound and text. The data may be stored in a variety of ways using conventional computer storage devices, together with a picture database on CD-ROM. Output might be through VDUs, sound-generators and laser projectors.

Integrating a tutor program could allow the system to be used as a training resource. The performance of the user could then be monitored by recording the choices made in response to questions and evaluating this response using an expert system. This performance output might then be sent to a remote trainer who would assess the trainee's progress.

Interactive video

involves the use of a computer linked to a large-capacity data store such as a Compact Disc (CD) to provide random access retrieval of images (including stills and continuous video) and sound. Data, once recorded, is not easily changed or added to and access times can sometimes appear long. However, any disadvantage arising is generally outweighed by the amount, variety and quality of data which can be retrieved from one active device.

HyperCard

including: card, stack
is an application-building tool provided with Apple Macintosh computers which allows for interactive storing and retrieving on-screen *'cards'*. These can contain text, graphics, sound and video clips, and are grouped together in one or more related *stacks*.

Browse

is a feature of hypertext systems which allows users to build their own route through an application rather than following a pre-determined one. The route so chosen may be remembered by the system so that it can be re-traced back to the starting point of that route. Browsers are particularly useful in such applications as computerised manuals, computer aided learning packages and large databases.

Video clip

is a short section of film or video stored in digital form (both sound and pictures). It is easily incorporated in computer displays and hypermedia systems. The video clip would normally be stored in compressed form, otherwise the storage cost would be prohibitive. See also *video data compression*, page 132.

A13   Computer Assisted Learning and Training

The foundations of computer assisted learning were laid during the early 1960s with the development of **programmed learning systems**. These early systems did not use any form of computer technology (the microcomputer was not to appear for many years) but were either paper-based or used electro-mechanical devices known as **teaching machines**.

A basic principle of programmed learning was one of 'value added'. Before any teaching programme was constructed, a pre-test and a post-test for the unit to be taught were written. A learner would sit the pre-test, undergo the programmed instruction and then sit the post-test. The value added to the learner could then be deduced by comparing the two scores. It was assumed that the learner could never be at fault. If the improvement in score was only small, then it was assumed that there was a problem with the programmed instruction.

The programmes could be either linear or branching. A **linear programme** would be a sequence of very small learning steps punctuated by a test question. The learner would know at once if they had answered correctly or not, but there would be no remedial instruction. A **branching programme** would not let the learner continue to the next step if a test answer was wrong. In this case one of several remedial instruction paths were followed depending on the nature of the error.

Some of the teaching machines were multimedia, controlling slide projectors and tape recorders. They were all expensive and unreliable. The paper form of the techniques were more successful. Books were written as branching programmes.

This approach to learning had some success with well defined skills or confined areas of training. The armed services based many of their instructional manuals on programmed learning principles and for a time it seemed that the Royal Air Force could have a significant influence on the educational system. Attempts to write programmes to deal with areas that required a creative and critical approach were poor and by the end of the 1960s interest in the approach had diminished.

Once the microcomputer arrived, the same principles were revived under the title of **Computer Aided Learning (CAL)**. Although now the technology was no longer a problem the learning programmes were just as difficult to write. The early CAL systems did little better than the programmed learning systems. One major useful contribution to learning was the development of *adventure* games. Another was the use of controllable computer simulations of situations which were too costly or too dangerous to create in real life. The general approach started to become effective when video and CD-ROM images could form part of the instructional material. It is now understood that an effective learning system must have the ability to adapt in a major way to the response of the learner. This can happen if the system is able to learn about the learner. **Expert systems** can do just this but, as with all effective software, they are expensive and difficult to write.

The processing speeds and data capacity of computers are ever increasing. Coupled with the development of even more adaptive software, it is to be expected that CAL will move onto the more creative areas of learning.

If the computer has so far proved to be limited in its role as a teacher it is much more effective as a manager of the learning process. **Computer Managed Learning (CML)** is very much concerned with the recording of what a learner has achieved and directing the learner to the next unit of study. Computers are good at recording well-structured data and making decisions based on well defined rules; CML is essentially recording and branching. The growth of a modular approach to learning courses has been made practical by the use of CML systems.

Authoring language
including: authoring system
is a programming language for the creation of instructional material that uses a *Computer Aided Learning* approach (see below). An ***authoring system*** is a computer system that is able to execute an authoring language.

Adventure game
is a computer game in which the player explores a computer-generated environment, usually having to solve puzzles in order to make progress. Early adventure games (named after the first one, which was called simply 'Adventure') used only text; the player typed instructions such as 'GO SOUTH', 'OPEN DOOR', 'PICK UP GOLD', and the computer responded with a description of the new scene. Later games make substantial use of graphics, and may be playable over a network with several players taking part.

Because of their problem-solving nature and the way in which they stimulate the imagination, adventure games have been widely and successfully used in education.

Computer Aided Learning (CAL)

including: Computer Based Training (CBT), Computer Managed Instruction (CMI), Computer Managed Learning (CML)

is the use of a computer to provide instructional information to a student, pose questions and react to the student's response.

Computer Based Training (CBT) is the use of a computer as an instructional system in a training environment. The approach is the same as computer assisted learning but the learning area is confined to a well defined training objective.

Computer Managed Instruction (CMI) is the use of a computer to manage a student's progress through a course of instruction. The student's performance is recorded by the computer and new modules of instruction are defined or delivered as determined by the curriculum. A computer managed instruction system may or may not contain computer assisted learning material.

Computer Managed Learning (CML) is the use of a computer in a similar fashion to computer managed instruction, but with additional emphasis on providing help which depends upon the responses given by the student. Some computer managed learning systems can build up a detailed learning profile for each student. This profile can be used for both reporting and directing the studies of an individual student.

Buggy

is a simple robotic device exclusively used in a computer education context. The device can move in two dimensions and supports light and touch *sensors* (see page 161). The student can program the device to exhibit certain behaviour or the device could form part of a multimedia *computer managed learning system* (see above).

Many buggies are controlled by an external general-purpose computer. This allows the use of a variety of programming languages to construct the controlling programs.

Turtle

is a simple robotic device initially designed to exploit the graphical aspects of the programming language LOGO (see page 174). It is designed to have a pen attached to it so that a hard copy of its walk can be recorded. Students can program the device with any suitable language but it could form part of a *computer managed learning system* (see above) associated with certain aspects of learning mathematics.

Roamer

including: Bigtrack

is a simple robotic device exclusively used in the computer education context. Unlike many *buggies* (see above) Roamer has a computer built into it. This computer controls the movement of Roamer by responding to a sequence of instructions. These instructions form a program which the student has stored in the device by the use of a set of keys which are part of Roamer. *Bigtrack* is a device that has a similar educational purpose to Roamer but it moves by laying tracks (like a tank) rather than wheels.

A14　Artificial Intelligence and Expert Systems

Artificial Intelligence (AI) is a recognised discipline within computer science. It attempts to design software (sometimes with associated hardware) that behaves in a way which, if it were human behaviour, would be described as intelligent.

The earliest artificial intelligence systems, in the 1960s, concentrated on such activities as playing chess and proving (mathematical) theorems. However the techniques built up are now being applied to aspects of behaviour not normally thought of as requiring great intelligence, such as recognising objects, understanding simple text, speech recognition and general visual interpretation.

These activities although often relatively straightforward for people are, in fact, not so straightforward for computers. It is a challenging problem to write programs for a computer to perform these activities - so much so that we are still far from successfully writing the programs, except in the most simple cases.

One recent development in artificial intelligence is neural networks. These draw from and emulate the structure of the brain in terms of neurons. The networks are made to 'learn' from training sessions and then repeat what has been learnt when given new data.

An **expert system**, sometimes known as an **Intelligent Knowledge Based System (IKBS)**, is an example of an 'intelligent' system applied to a real life application. The computer performs at or near the level of human experts.

Examples of expert systems include PROSPECTOR, which advises geologists when they are out in the field. The system asks for certain data about the environment where the geologist is considering drilling bore-holes and provides advice based on this data and on 'knowledge' already stored in its knowledge base.

Other well known expert systems include XCON, which gives advice on how to configure a VAX computer system – that is , how to make sure the correct units are specified and how they should be connected together for a certain application. There are a number of systems in the medical area; one of the better known is MYCIN, which gives advice on which drugs to use for certain types of bacterial infection.

Artificial Intelligence (AI)

is the study and development of computing applications for tasks which would be described as requiring intelligence, if they were done by people. Many of these applications involve systems capable of learning, adaptation or self-correction.

Cognitive science

covers a wide range of subjects which are concerned with the thinking processes (cognition) and are, to a great extent, people-oriented. Some, such as *artificial intelligence* (see above), computer vision and *human-computer interaction* (see page 71), are concerned with computers. Others are concerned with how people function; for example, cognitive psychology which includes the study of the mental processes of memory, language processing and vision. Some cognitive scientists find it helpful to describe how humans function in terms of a computer model of information processing.

Neural net

is artificial intelligence software which allows a system to learn to recognise features or characteristics of situations which are input to it. The technique is based on a model of the logical properties of interconnected sets of nerve cells.

A neural net is made up of a network of very many junctions, or nodes. Each of these nodes will 'learn' features according to its input. Once the learning phase is completed, the neural net can be used to recognise features of the same type that were presented to it.

Neural nets have been used for visual recognition and also for financial prediction.

Pattern recognition

is the process of identifying objects in a digitised picture, or in some cases digitised sounds, through analysis of the digital representation of the objects and comparison with stored knowledge about similar objects.

Cybernetics

including: robotics

is the study of the control of processes by a computer, for example an industrial process or a robot. *Robotics* is the study and design of robots. See also *control,* page 38, and *robot,* page 40.

Expert system

also known as: (Intelligent) Knowledge Based System (IKBS), (KBS)
including: knowledge base, knowledge engineer, knowledge acquisition,
knowledge elicitation, inference engine, heuristics, explanation, rulebase,
shell

is an application of artificial intelligence to a particular area of activity where traditional human expert knowledge and experience are made available through a computer package.

Knowledge base is that part of an expert system which holds knowledge about the application area (or domain), such as drug side effects. Much of the knowledge is held as **IF ... THEN ...** type rules. For example:

```
IF a patient has high blood pressure
AND is anaemic
THEN avoid the use of a certain kind of
drug.
```

From time to time the knowledge base is updated.

Heuristics are rules which are not derived purely from logic but are derived from the experience of a person. These are known as 'rules of thumb'. Many of the rules in an expert system are of this type.

Rulebase is the part of the knowledge base which is made up of all the rules known to the expert system.

Knowledge engineers are the people who collect the information in the knowledge base. This information is collected from a variety of sources in a variety of ways; one of the most important is collecting information through talking to experts. The collected knowledge is then formulated as a set of rules and facts.

Knowledge acquisition or *knowledge elicitation* is the process of gathering information for inclusion in a knowledge base.

Once the knowledge base has been constructed, the expert system is ready to be interrogated or consulted. The system requests the user to provide information and then searches the knowledge base to find appropriate advice for the user.

Explanations can be requested by the user. The system will provide the user with the reasoning behind the advice given. This is often in the form of a list of the rules tested by the system.

Inference engine (or *inference processor*) is a piece of software in an expert system which does the searching of the knowledge base. Searching the knowledge base uses standard searching methods which are independent of the application, for example a top-down or a bottom-up search.

Shell is a piece of software, which is an 'empty' expert system without the knowledge base for any particular application. The user enters the appropriate rules and facts.

Expert systems have a clearly identifiable internal structure, which is illustrated in Figure A14.1.

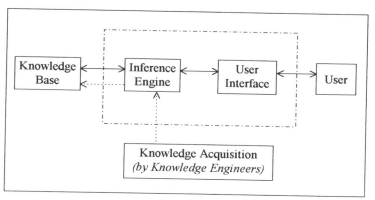

Figure A14.1: An expert system structure

The user communicates with the system through the User Interface, which passes requests for advice to the Inference Engine. The Inference Engine processes the request, obtaining information – rules and facts – from the Knowledge Base as required and finally returns the answer to the User Interface, and hence to the user.

In the Knowledge Acquisition phase, the Inference Engine stores the information from the Knowledge Engineers in the Knowledge Base.

A15   User Interface

Cooks usually try to make their meals tasty and attractive as well as nutritious. In the same way, software writers try to make their products attractive to the user as well as being effective and easy to use. Much time and effort is spent on designing ways in which the user interacts with the computer and the software. Most software users are more concerned with what a package can do than with how it works. They expect to be able to see and understand what the software can do, they want to be able to communicate their instructions easily and have quick and understandable responses from the computer.

As the scope of computer applications has increased and the number of computer users has also increased, a variety of ways have been evolved for communication between the user and the computer; this is called the **user interface** or **user environment**. There are fashions in user interface design, just as there are in car or clothes design, but what is important is that the interface should achieve its objectives as efficiently as possible.

All user interface designs are limited by the capabilities of machines and people. Each design seeks to make the most of the strengths and avoid the weaknesses of computer equipment and its users. Aspects of computer hardware, for example processing speed, memory capacity, input and output devices, restrict what software can achieve. Speech is the most common form of communication between people but the development of methods of communication between people and computers through speech has not yet produced cheap and reliable systems for everyday use. Communication through text is limited by the speed at which people can read text which is presented on a screen and type responses accurately on a keyboard. Recent improvements in hardware have greatly enhanced the graphics capability of small computers. Many software designers have chosen graphical ways of presenting the activities or concepts available for selection at any time: icons (small pictures with an easily understood meaning) are widely used, since graphical information is independent of the user's language and can be used wherever the meaning of the icon is understood. All user interface designs are compromises between what it is desirable to provide and what it is possible to achieve.

It is the combination of those parts of the hardware and software of a system with which the user interacts which make up the user interface. User interfaces are described in a variety of ways, whose names highlight their main features; for example, **graphical user interface (GUI), menu selection**

interface, windows environment, forms dialogue. There is no single kind of user environment which suits all applications or all users; the choice of an appropriate user interface depends on the amount of information to be presented or elicited, the experience of the users and their familiarity with the particular software.

Since taste and personal preference largely determine people's reactions to different user environments, there will always be scope for variety in their design. For those people who spend a long time working at a computer it is very important that the user interface they experience makes a positive contribution to their efficiency. It is increasingly common for the user to be able to adapt (**customise**) the facilities provided by the system to fit the situation in which the system is used.

Where there is an unusual user environment, such as where provision has to be made for disabled people, special arrangements are often made. These may include the provision of customised input and/or output devices, such as touch sensitive keyboards, and the appropriate additional software.

Human-Computer Interaction (HCI)
sometimes: interface rather than interaction
including: Man-Machine Interface (MMI), user interface, user environment, Graphical User Interface (GUI)
is one of a number of terms used to describe the communication between people and computer systems. Other terms for this are: ***Man-Machine Interface (MMI)***, ***user interface*** and ***user environment***. Any of these terms is likely to be used in discussions of how people and computer systems interact and the ease of use of a system.

One way of classifying interfaces is by the style of communication they provide. Some are purely textual whilst others, known as ***Graphical User Interfaces (GUI)***, replace some or all of the words by icons. See also the introduction to this section.

Keyboard
including: qwerty keyboard, numeric keypad, function key, embedded keyboard
is the typical input device used with all general-purpose computers. A keyboard will have a number of keys, which is not the same for all computers nor is the arrangement the same.

Part of the keyboard is likely to be arranged in the same way as a traditional typewriter; this is called a ***qwerty keyboard.***

Part of the keyboard may be a block of keys for the digits 0-9, possibly including the arithmetic symbols for add, subtract, multiply and divide, and an enter key; this is called a *numeric keypad*.

In addition to the keys for letters, numbers and punctuation marks, a typical keyboard will have special keys including, at least, enter (or return), escape (esc), control (ctrl) and some *function keys*. What these keys do will de₁ end on the software being used rather than the hardware.

It is sometimes possible for the user to assign part of the keyboard for special purposes. This part of the keyboard is called an *embedded keyboard*. For example, keyboards with a restricted number of keys, such as laptop computers, allow a group of the keys to be assigned the role of a numeric keypad if the user wishes.

WIMP environment (Windows Icons Menus Pointer)

is a method of accessing the computer making minimum use of the keyboard by using a *mouse* (or similar device) to move a *pointer* over *icons* or text *menus* displayed on the screen. For example, selecting an icon may open a *window* and start a task. For definitions of these individual terms see below.

Window

including: active window, pane

is a temporary area opened on the screen displaying the activity of a program. There can be several windows on the screen at any one time which can be moved if required or removed completely (restoring the original information on the screen). At any one time only one window will be *active*, that is accessible for input by the user. Things may be happening in other windows, for example a clock may be showing the time, but this does not mean that the window is active. If several activities are being run at the same time, each will be in a separate window but only one can be worked on at a time. It is possible to have more than one window visible and shift from one task to another by moving the cursor from one window to another. A window may be divided into parts, called *panes*, which can be used separately; for example headers and footers in a document.

Highlighting
including: inverse video
is changing the appearance of a part of a screen display by altering it in some
way so that it stands out; for example by changing colour arrangements or by
putting shading around an area of the screen. One commonly used method
involves the use of *inverse video*, in which black becomes white and colours
change to the colour represented by the inverse bit pattern, for example the
inverse of 00011011 is 11100100.

Highlighting changes:

HIGHLIGHT   into   **HIGHLIGHT**

Mouse
including: mouse button, mouse event
is a computer input device, usually connected to the computer by a thin cable.
Using a hand to move the mouse in contact with a flat surface causes a cursor,
or pointer, on the display screen to move. A mouse has one, or more, finger-
operated press switches, called *(mouse) buttons*. When a mouse button is
pressed it causes a 'click' sound and passes a signal to the computer; the same
thing happens when the switch is released. What effect these have will depend
upon where the pointer is on the screen and what software is being used.
Mouse operations, such as *clicking* (see below), dragging (see *drag*, below) or
combining these with the use of keys on the keyboard provide a wide range of
possible options at any moment. Actions, such as pressing or releasing the
mouse buttons, are sometimes called *mouse events*. One alternative to a
mouse is a *trackerball* (see below).

Trackerball
sometimes called: trackball
is an input device which is used to do the same things as a *mouse* (see above).
It is a ball, set into a cup, which can be made to roll in any direction by using
a finger or the palm of a hand, depending on the size of the ball. The
movements of the ball are mirrored on the screen by a pointer and finger-
operated switches work in the same way as *mouse buttons* (see above).
Trackerballs are now sometimes mounted on *laptop computers* (see page 101),
being easier to use in this position than a mouse.

Clicking

including: double clicking

Pressing a mouse button is called clicking, because this usually produces a 'click' sound. If the user clicks when the pointer controlled by the mouse is on an *icon* (see above), or a *screen button* (see below), then the operation represented by that icon (or button) is selected. For example, clicking on the picture of the flag of a country may cause its national anthem to be played.

Some software expects the mouse button to be pressed twice in quick succession which is called **double clicking**; a single click may have one effect while double clicking may have another.

Dialogue box

including: text box, list box

is a window which appears when information about a choice is needed, or when options have to be selected. For example, choosing PRINT from a FILE menu may cause a dialogue box to appear, requiring answers to such questions as the name of the file, how many copies, etc. Normally, a dialogue box will offer the chance to cancel the request as well as the option to proceed. Dialogue boxes are intended to make it easy to obtain the necessary information quickly.

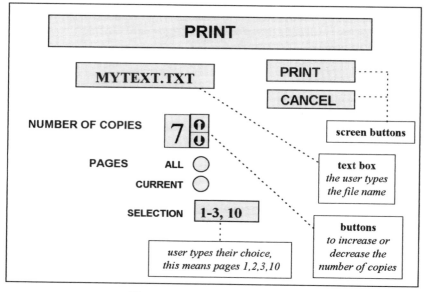

Figure A15.1: *Dialogue box*

In the dialogue box, shown in Figure A15.1, the *text box* for typing the file name, **MYTEXT.TXT**, could be replaced by a *list box*, in which the application shows a list of file names from which the user selects with the pointer.

Some list boxes stay the same size, others drop down to show several items.

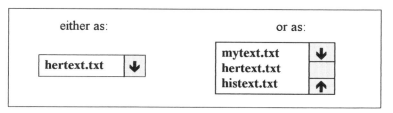

Figure A15.2: List box

See also the diagram, Figure A15.5, in *conversational interface,* page 80.

Screen button

is the name given to an area of the screen which is used to select an action. Selection is usually achieved by moving the pointer to the button and then pressing (and releasing) a *mouse button* (see above). A screen button may be an icon or the picture of a button switch with an icon or a word on it. See also *toolbar,* below, and *dialogue box,* above.

Drag

including: drag-and-drop editing
is the use of a mouse (or other similar device) to move an area of a screen display, which may be text or some part of a graphic display, bodily from one location to another. Before such movement can take place, the area concerned has to be defined in some way such as *highlighting* text (see above), or marking the boundaries of a graphics item. Moving things around in this way is sometimes referred to as ***drag-and-drop editing,*** which may also be used to copy, as well as move, part of a screen display. One example of dragging is moving the icon for a file from one sub-directory to another as a way of repositioning the file within the directory; another would be moving a graphic item from an application running in one window on the screen to a different application running in another window. Drag is sometimes used to mean moving the mouse while holding down a button.

Scrolling

including: scroll bar

is the action of 'rolling-up' a screen. As each new line appears at the bottom, the existing top line disappears off the top. Where an application occupies more than a single screen, it is usual to provide a *scroll bar* to move the displayed portion of the application up or down the screen (vertical scrolling) and sometimes left and right across the screen (horizontal scrolling, see Figure A15.3).

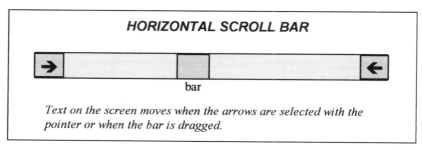

HORIZONTAL SCROLL BAR

bar

Text on the screen moves when the arrows are selected with the pointer or when the bar is dragged.

Figure A15.3: *Scroll bar*

Toolbar

including: tool, toggle

is a line of *screen buttons* (see above) which represent the actions, *tools,* that are currently available to be carried out within an applications package or a system. For example, clicking on an icon for a brush in a drawing program will select a paintbrush tool. It is normal to make the icons behave like press switches (buttons), so that it is possible to see which tool has been selected or if the tool is still selected. Clicking on a selected tool again will cancel the selection; this means that the switches are *toggles*, changing each time they are 'clicked'.

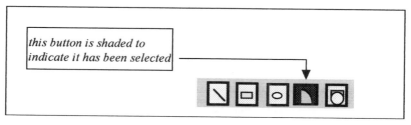

this button is shaded to indicate it has been selected

Figure A15.4: *Toolbar*

Toolbox is sometimes used to describe a collection of *utility programs* (see page 172).

Hot key

also known as: quick key

is a function key or a key combination (frequently combining *control* or *alt* with other keys), which causes an action (such as calling up a menu, or running another program) whatever the user is doing. The name suggests the urgency of beginning a new action without fully breaking off from the existing task, or without the need to progress through a sequence of menus. The uses of *function keys* (see page 72) are sometimes defined as a menu on the screen or may be defined on a *keystrip* (see page 88) for the application.

Macro recording

is the action of recording a sequence of keystrokes, which achieve a particular purpose, and saving the recording for future use. By assigning a *hot key* (see above) to stand for this recorded sequence it is possible to make frequently required actions easier to perform. For example, a single key combination could be used to type the whole of a frequently used phrase.

Interactive computing

including: conversational mode

is a mode of operation in which the user and a computer system are in two-way communication throughout the period of use. In practice, most personal computer applications are interactive, whereas some applications on terminals attached to large central computer systems, for example in supermarket branches, are still run in batch mode with data and command instructions supplied through the terminal. When a terminal user on a network appears to be in continuous communication with the central computer, getting replies almost immediately, it is described as *conversational mode*.

Command line interface

including: command sequence

is a form of user interface in which the user types commands for the computer to carry out. As the term suggests, the command is usually restricted to a single line of text, which may consist of any sequence of acceptable commands. The user has to know the conventions used in the commands. These commands may be combined to make up a *command sequence*, which can make this a convenient way of getting the computer to perform a sequence of actions (see *macro recording*, above). This form of interface can be efficient in the hands of experienced users, but can be very frustrating for those who do not know the right commands to use.

Conversational interface

is a form of user interface in which the computer and the user appear to be holding a conversation or dialogue, using the screen for output and the keyboard for input. The user may be seeking information from the computer, but the computer may need to ask its own questions before it is able to provide the answer to the question originally asked. The example below, which could be a dialogue about a request to print a file, gives an indication of the kind of communication that might be experienced:

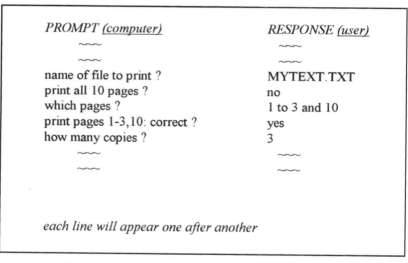

Figure A15.5: Conversational dialogue screen

Forms dialogue interface

including: response field

is a user interface in which the computer outputs separate *prompt* (see below) and response fields for a number of inputs.

Response field is the place in a dialogue screen (Figure A15.6) where users may type their responses, in any order. There may be automatic movement of the cursor, depicting the entry point, from response field to response field. The process is similar to filling in a form on paper and allows the entries to be changed at any stage until the 'execution' key or button is pressed.

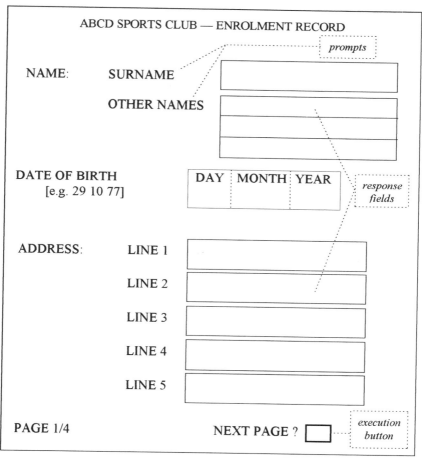

Figure A15.6: Forms dialogue screen

Wildcard

is a symbol used in some commands or search instructions to stand for a range of characters. For example, `?` is often used to stand for any single character, hence the command `type d????.doc` would cause all files of type `.doc` whose names have five characters beginning with a `d` to be typed. The character `*` is usually used to stand for any group of characters (or perhaps none), hence the command `delete *.*` may be unwise, since it could cause all files to be deleted.

Directory

including: sub-directory, directory file, folder
is a group of files or a group of files and ***sub-directories***. A sub-directory is a directory within a directory, its contents may be files or other sub-directories or both. A directory is held, in the form of a list of file and sub-directory names (the ***directory file***), on the backing store to which it refers; stored with it will be information needed for files to be retrieved from the backing store. A directory file is sometimes referred to as a ***folder***. Directories are usually represented in a tree structure (see *tree*, page 27), as shown in Figure A15.7. See also *file*, page 179.

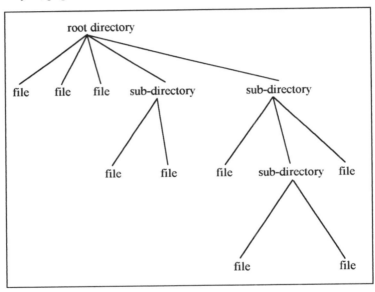

Figure A15.7: *Directory tree*

Error message

is a message to the user indicating that something has gone wrong; it may include instructions on what action is needed. Well designed applications packages will include comprehensive error detection routines and helpful error messages. These routines will detect errors resulting from user mistakes, such as letting the printer run out of paper or failing to put the right disk into a disk drive, as well as errors occurring in the system itself.

Password

including: logging in (log in, logging on, log on), logging out (log out, logging off, log off), personal identification device, (PID), personal identification number, (PIN)

is the sequence of characters, known only to the user and the computer system, that must be presented as part of *logging in* to a computer system with security protection before it will allow a user access to the system. Some parts of the system may have additional passwords.

Logging in (*also known as: log in, logging on, log on*) is the procedure that has to be followed to gain access to and begin a session on a multi-access system with security procedures.

Logging out (*also known as: log out, logging off, log off*) is the correct procedure to be followed when ending a session on a multi-access system.

In addition to using passwords, some systems also have some kind of 'electronic key', such as a cash card for bank systems, which has to be used with a password. This is sometimes referred to as a *personal identification device (PID)*.

Personal identification number (PIN) is a number used as a password, particularly with cash cards used in cash points (see *automatic teller machines,* page 20).

Prompt

is a character or message displayed on a screen to indicate that the user is expected to do something, usually to input data into the system. Sometimes a visual prompt is emphasised by a sound.

Screen editing

is the process of changing (editing) stored data or programs using a computer screen. The characters which are the data or programs are altered on the screen by adding, removing or changing individual characters or groups of characters.

Smart card

is a plastic card in the same format (the same size and shape) as a credit card which has a microprocessor and memory built into it. It has much greater memory than the magnetic stripe on a normal plastic card.

Light pen

is an input device, which looks like a pen with a wire connecting it to the computer. The light pen is used to point at, and thus indicate, a position on the screen. Software is used to calculate this position and perform an appropriate action. One application is the use of the pen to draw on the screen rather like an artist drawing on paper.

Touch sensitive keyboard

including: concept keyboard

is a type of keyboard in which the 'keys' are sensitive areas of a plastic surface. These keyboards are generally used in special situations, for example where there is a risk of dirt or liquids getting into a conventional keyboard. Overlays are put on the keyboard to indicate the areas and their meaning, and software interprets this for the computer. One particular kind of touch sensitive keyboard is called a *concept keyboard*. This has programmable areas to input information to the computer. It is often used with young or disabled learners.

Touchpad

also known as: touch switch, pressure pad, pressure switch

is one of a number of names for *touch* or *pressure* operated sensor *pads* or *switches*, used as input devices for some applications. They can be used in conjunction with special software to enable people with severe physical disabilities to select items displayed on a screen by touching (or pressing) the pad when the item needed is highlighted. See also *touch sensitive keyboard,* above.

Touchscreen

is a special screen that is able to detect the position on the screen which a user's finger is touching or pointing at. One way of doing this is by having two sets of fine wires on the screen (one set across and the other down) which sense the finger position. Another way is to have vertical and horizontal patterns of infra red light beams which are interrupted when a finger (or pointer) is close to the screen. With both these methods, the software can calculate what position has been touched.

User friendly

describes a system, either hardware or software, which is kind to its users. Since the user interface largely determines what a user experiences, it is the software system which is generally being described. However, some aspects of hardware, such as the feel of a keyboard, can improve or spoil user friendliness.

User transparent

sometimes: transparency

describes actions by a computer system, hardware or software, which are not obvious to the user. Nearly all hardware actions, other than those affecting the screen, are transparent, and most operating system actions take place without the user being aware of them. Well designed user interfaces achieve high levels of *transparency*.

Wizard

is a feature of some applications packages, which helps users to perform a task. By asking the user some questions, a wizard provides help in making best use of the available facilities. For example, a table wizard might help to create tables by offering a number of possible types, or a letter wizard might show how you could set out a letter for a particular situation.

A16   *User Documentation*

Other terms related to documentation will be found in
B9 Systems Documentation. As User Documentation is
concerned with making the computer easy to use, terms in
section A15 User Interface may also be of interest.

Software Documentation

When a computer software package is bought, whether it is a computer
game, a spreadsheet or a programming language, user documentation will also
be received. This may be anything from an instruction leaflet to a series of
manuals. This 'user documentation' is designed to introduce the package and
to tell the user how to use the software to its best advantage. This
documentation may be totally in printed form or it may be seen on the screen
when running the package. There may also be files on the accompanying disks
called "Readme" or "Help".

There must be an overview of the package describing what it is capable of
doing in fairly broad terms but also include some specific uses and features
that are important with this package. This may include some sample screen
displays and printouts to show the users what to expect.

An early section should be on how to install the software (to make the
software available on the user's system). These instructions might well
include

- how to make extra copies of disks for safety (in case the working disk is
  damaged)
- how to copy on to a hard disk and configure the software (where the
  user has a choice of options as to how the software is to work and what
  hardware will be used, such as the type of printer)
- how to make hardware adjustments that may be needed. These may be
  described for the user to do or may require the help of a dealer.

Some of these operations may refer to hardware documentation. For
example reference may be needed to printer documentation.

It may be that the software has already been installed, so installation and
configuration may not seem to be of interest. However, if the printer is
changed, the configuration process will probably need repeating, either by the
user or the supplier.

It is important that the novice user has access to tutorial material consisting
of written instructions or similar sequences given as an on-screen tutorial.
This is designed to speed the user through the simple aspects onto the more

advanced usage that may have been in mind when the purchase was made. Equally for the more experienced user there should be some summary sheet or quick reference guide. It is useful to have a reference to the use of specific keys (such as the function keys), perhaps in the form of a **keystrip** (a piece of card or plastic that is fitted onto the keyboard).

One of the first actions of the user should be to register the purchase with the publishing software company so that any upgrade or fault information can be passed on. With more sophisticated packages there might be a telephone help line.

An index to the documentation should help the user to find how to do specific tasks and to find more detailed explanations of error messages.

Hardware Documentation

Any piece of hardware will need some instructions on how to use it. Usually a physical connection will need to be made between items of equipment, for example between a monitor and computer. This will specify details of the connecting leads and where they are to be connected.

Most computers can have 'add on' peripherals, such as scanners or hard drives, to attach to existing systems. Some hardware needs minor physical adjustment before connecting it to a computing system. Some hardware devices are attached via a SCSI (Small Computer Systems Interface) and these devices need a unique device number. These could be set by use of jumpers. Printers commonly have switches which are controlled *either* by software *or* by hardware. **DIP switches** (see Figure A16.2 for an example) are commonly used to specify the details of paper to be used, the characters to be printed and the type and speed of communication between computer and printer. These details may alternatively be specified by a special sequence of key presses on the device. Printers also may need to have paper feed mechanisms fitted.

With a new computer system the user documentation will also give the options that are controlled by software. These might include the type of monitor to be used, the type of printer and the speed of response of the mouse. Instructions on using the mouse, general care of the computer and use of disk drives are usually included. These will include how to format and copy disks and precautions that should be taken to prevent accidental damage and loss of data. Documentation may contain details on how your hardware may be customised for improving performance in a variety of circumstances. There is often a section on troubleshooting faults should your system not respond as it should, for example what to do if the printer produces gibberish or the screen remains blank.

More technical detail is usually available (at extra cost) from the manufacturer or a third party. The quality of such literature varies in its accuracy and clarity.

Keystrip

is a piece of card or plastic used with a keyboard. It labels the operations performed by function keys within specific programs. For example, in a word processor the function key F4 might have Search/Replace above it (see Figure A16.1).

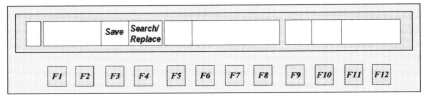

Figure A16.1: A keystrip

Tutorial

provides the user with a guided tour through the software. It is a sequence of tasks to be carried out. This will help the user to find out how to use the software by experimenting with it and seeing the results.

User documentation

gives the user any information necessary for the successful running of a piece of software or hardware. This does not generally include many technical details which will usually be found in *maintenance documentation*, page 170.

README file

is a file which is provided on the medium with the software. It contains the latest details of using or loading the software.

HELP system

is a means of providing helpful messages to guide a user when using a software package. It will give indications of how to answer prompts from the software and how to perform relevant operations.

DIP switch

is one of a set of small slide operated switches mounted together in a bank (Figure A16.2). These are used to set options on hardware, such as printers.

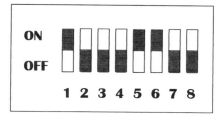

Figure A16.2: *Bank of eight DIP switches*

Jumper

is a detachable flexible-wire connection between suitable socket points on a circuit board. Sometimes a rigid version may be found on printers and other peripherals, possibly arranged in banks like *DIP switches* (see above), for which they are an alternative.

Install

is to transfer software onto the medium from which it is to be run. Installation is normally onto a hard drive but could be onto a floppy disk or a network.

Deinstall

including: key disk

is to remove software from a medium, the process is the reverse of *install*. This should remove all traces of the software and release the space from the storage medium. If the license is to install a limited number of copies, then deinstallation recredits the disk (normally called the *key disk*, see below).

Control panel

is a small display/keyboard on a device that enables the user to set options. On a printer this may be used to set the print style or change the paper source.

Key disk

is a disk used to install software which contains credits that are reduced by one on each installation. It may also be a disk that is required every time a program is run to reduce the possibility of software piracy. See also *software copyright*, page 97.

Dongle

is a piece of hardware used to reduce the possibility of software piracy. It usually plugs into a standard interface on a computer. Without the correct dongle the protected software will not run.

A17   Computer Personnel

*Further definitions related to the area of human-computer
interaction are found in section A15 User Interface.*

Computer systems are the concern of people and human-computer interaction
is extensive.

It is people who ask for systems, specify systems, design and build
systems. They develop and enhance existing systems, implement systems,
manage and use systems. People – as described through their personal
information – are often both the direct source and the subject of the computer's
database. The demand, by people, for information is the main reason why
computers are needed.

In many organisations, the 1990s have seen an increase in both the number
and the types of task which computers have been required to perform. To
enable this expansion of use to be managed in a controlled and professional
manner, not only have computer-related job descriptions and responsibilities
changed but many jobs on the user side of the interface have similarly been
affected.

This section gives an indication of the types of job related to computer use
and offers a brief description of some of those jobs. A more detailed
description of the wide range of IT (information technology) jobs, and the skill
levels involved, can be obtained by examining the British Computer Society's
Industry Structure Model.

Recently, some large organisations have changed their operational methods
and, instead of employing teams of IT specialists themselves, have signed
contracts with outside firms who agree to supply these specialist staff as and
when required. This is known as **outsourcing**.

Computer support personnel

are those involved in the day-to-day running of an organisation's computing
installation.

Computer operator

is the person who operates the computer and, where appropriate, responds to
requests from the operating system and from remote users in a time-sharing
system.

Data processing manager

is the person responsible for the overall running of a data processing department.

Database administrator

is the person in an organisation responsible for the structure and control of the data in the organisation's database. See also *database management system*, page 26.

Decision support specialist

is responsible for organising database interrogation procedures to allow business managers to access management information in appropriate formats.

Network controller

also known as: network manager

is the person responsible for the smooth running of a network. This will generally include communications (software and hardware), access (user identifications and passwords) and shared resources such as common data storage. (Compare with *network controller - types of computer*, page 104.)

Data preparation staff

are those responsible for organising and entering data into the computer system.

Hybrid manager

combines business understanding, IT technical competence and organisational knowledge and skills. Typically, the IT skills component will be gained after the acquisition of the business and organisational components.

Programmer

including: systems programmer, applications programmer, information systems engineer, coder

is the person responsible for writing and testing computer programs. Those involved in the writing of operating systems, general utilities (such as sort routines) and specialist tools (such as a graphical user interface) are usually called **systems programmers**, while those writing programs for specific user applications are known as **applications programmers**.

Those programmers working on the design and testing of programs are often called **information systems engineers**, while those who are mostly involved in translating statements into machine readable form are called **coders**.

Systems analyst/systems designer

is the person responsible for the analysis of a system to assess its suitability for computerisation. Where computerisation is decided upon, the systems designer will be responsible for building on the analyst's results to create the new computer-based system and will normally work up to the point where programmers can sensibly take over.

Where persons who have been responsible for the analysis then work on the new system design, they are referred to as *analyst/designers*.

Technical support staff

are computer specialists who are concerned with the integrity and functionality of the computer system. They may be hardware rather than software oriented.

Computer service engineer

also known as: computer engineer, maintenance engineer, service engineer
is the person responsible for the maintenance of the hardware, and is often employed by a specialist contract servicing company.

Software support staff

including: help desk, hot line
are usually employed by software houses or specialist vendors in order to respond to questions relating to the use of particular pieces of software. They are often referred to as a '*help desk*' and may be contacted quickly using the telephone '*hot line*' to give advice on problem solving.

Information systems manager

is the current term for the person who manages the interface between the computer system and the organisation's user community.

Data Protection Officer

is the named person in an organisation who is responsible for seeing that the organisation's registration (under the *UK Data Protection Act 1984*, see page 95) is adhered to.

Outsourcing

is the principle of buying-in information systems services from specialist organisations instead of continuing the traditional practice of retaining company employees to provide them.

Industry Structure Model (ISM)

Designed by the British Computer Society, this sets out, as a series of competences, what is expected of a person performing computer-related tasks at each stage in a variety of career paths.

Computer systems contain valuable and meaningful data. The accuracy, currency, integrity and accessibility of data form the basis of reliable output. Safeguarding this data is vital both to the owner and to the user of the data.

Incorrect data can result in inappropriate output. Actions based on that output can be costly. Damage can be caused to machines controlled by such output and the reputation, health or livelihood of people can be put at risk.

In the United Kingdom, and also in many other countries, there is legislation which covers the use of a variety of data processing activities with severe penalties for breaking these laws. Therefore, safeguarding data makes sense for both economic and legal reasons.

Computer systems in manufacturing, real-time processes and safety critical applications may need to meet certain design standards and their implementation may need to conform to quality assurance standards. Product Liability legislation, particularly in the USA, imposes severe penalties on the producers of poor quality computing products.

There is also legislation covering copyright which enables software producers to protect their investment in software development.

Computer Misuse Act
including: computer abuse
is the 1990 United Kingdom Act of Parliament aimed specifically at 'hackers'. It defines *computer misuse* as the unauthorised use of computer systems and relates both to hardware (using a particular computer without permission) and software (accessing parts of the system without authorisation). It introduced three new offences relating to unauthorised computer access and to unauthorised modification or deletion of data.

Computer abuse is not legally defined, but is generally taken to be the wrongful use of computer systems and software for improper anti-social or illegal purposes, including fraud, the propagation of *viruses* (see below), data terrorism (threats made against computer systems and data) and computer pornography.

Data protection
including: Data Protection Act
is the establishment of safeguards to preserve integrity, privacy and security of data.

Data Protection Act is the 1984 United Kingdom Act of Parliament which sets out requirements for the control of personal data stored on computer systems. The Act covers many aspects of data protection. It also requires that data users attend to such matters as the accuracy and appropriateness of the data they hold. The right of individuals to see – and where necessary to correct – personal data is also covered. Data users covered under the Act are required to supply, to a public register, sufficient details about themselves and the nature, purpose and range of the data they hold. This information should enable any individual to ascertain if personal data relating to them is likely to be held by that data user. If a data user holds personal data about an individual, that individual can require the data user to supply a copy of that data.

Hacking

is the term used to describe attempts (successful or otherwise) to gain unauthorised access to computer systems. This may relate to the unauthorised use of a computer or to unauthorised access to particular programs or data stored on that computer (for example, by persons who exceed the legitimate permissions which they may have to use only part of a total system).

Integrity

describes the consistency of data during and after processing. Data which has not been accidentally or maliciously corrupted is said to have integrity.

Piracy

is the illegal copying of software whether for personal use or re-sale.

Privacy

is the recognition of the private nature of certain data which should only be accessed by, or disclosed to, an authorised person. In considering the maintenance of privacy, systems designers build safeguards into both operational routines (for example, the use of *passwords*, see page 83) and physical areas (for example, the use of *personal identification devices*, see page 83) to allow systems controllers to reduce the risks of unauthorised access.

Security

is the establishment and application of safeguards to protect data, software and computer hardware from accidental or malicious modification, destruction or (in the case of data) unauthorised disclosure.

Encryption

is the encoding of data by a computer system. Its purpose is to add a level of security to the data, both when stored electronically and when being transmitted between computer systems. To provide the correct output, matching encoding and decoding algorithms need to be used.

In conventional systems the same cipher key is used for both the enciphering and deciphering stages and therefore all users must have a copy of the key. Where the number of users is small and the concern is for security of stored data, a single cipher key is usually sufficient. Where transmission, rather than storage, requires extra protection it is possible to have different enciphering and deciphering keys. See *public key cryptography*, page 44, and *data encryption standard*, page 43.

Electronic signature

is a specific code related to a particular operation or data set, which needs to be matched by an input signal, before that operation can be authorised or before that data set can be addressed.

Virus

including: worm,, Trojan, computer hygiene, virus checking, disinfection
is a routine which is designed to alter any other routine if a particular pre-determined set of conditions occurs. The design of viruses often includes an instruction to replicate itself under some other pre-determined set of conditions. Most viruses are specific to some particular host (such as a boot program) but others, once activated, can replicate spontaneously (this type may be called a *worm*) or perform their illegal objective (called a *Trojan* or *Trojan Horse*).

Virus problems may be dealt with by the use of proprietary software designed to detect and remove a wide variety of them (often this software is marketed under the heading of *computer hygiene*). The process of detecting viruses already in the system is usually called *virus checking*.

Some computer hygiene programs may be placed resident in memory and continually monitor executable files for changes in size. If any change is detected, the file is prevented from being run and a user message is given. New data read into the computer is also screened for viruses and appropriate action taken. These actions are known as *disinfection*.

Software copyright

including: software licence, FAST (Federation Against Software Theft), freeware, shareware

It is not always realised that computer software is covered by similar copyright laws to those which apply to books and other publications. The 1988 Copyright, Designs and Patents Act protects 'intellectual property' and establishes the rights of the author. The unauthorised use of any commercial software that has not been properly purchased with a *software licence* is illegal. In practice, this means that copying software bought by someone else is likely to be an offence. Even the use of properly-purchased software on a network can be illegal unless the licence specifically allows this form of multiple use. See also *key disk,* page 89.

*FAST (**Federation Against Software Theft**)* is an organisation operating on behalf of software producers; it actively pursues breaches of software copyright. Sometimes, however, software is offered copyright-free; this may be called *freeware* or *shareware.*

Part B:
What Computer Systems Are Made Of

Computer systems can be assembled out of a variety of different pieces of hardware and software in many different arrangements. This part of the glossary defines terms which will be encountered when considering how computer systems are arranged, organised and connected to other computer systems. It also includes terms involved with the design and use of software. Terms related to the uses of computer systems are in Part A.

B1 *Types of Computer*

This section includes those terms that are descriptive of computers in general.

A computer is an automatic, programmable, digital data processor. Every part of this definition is crucial to our understanding of what the modern computer is, and how it works. **Automatic** means simply that it operates without human intervention, except where this is expressly pre-planned and provided for. This feature alone distinguishes the computer from the simple pocket calculator, where each computation results from a manual key-press. **Programmable** means that the instructions to be followed automatically are held (as a 'program') within the store of the computer. If a repetitive calculation (a 'loop') is necessary, the same instructions can be used and re-used. The instructions are usually held in the same storage area as that used for data – computer programs and the data they operate on can comfortably co-exist in the same sort of storage. Often (usually), the instructions can be replaced with other instructions: either as a part of developing a program to completion, or as a wholesale replacement of one program with another. **Digital** means that the computer operates with quantities that take only distinct values from a known range: often, but not always, these are binary quantities that take only two values, 'on' and 'off'. The power of digital data is that the computer (and the programmer) knows in advance what the data will look like: this is very similar to the human knowledge that all numbers, no matter how large, can be expressed as a combination of the ten digits 0, 1, 2, 3, ... 9. In principle, humans can add together (or multiply, divide – whatever) *any* two numbers. The 'hundreds, tens and units' method can easily be extended to numbers as large as we please. Notice that, because programs and data can occupy the same storage in the computer, programs are also expressed digitally. Although digital processing is now almost universal, computers did not always work this way – see *analog computer* below.

Finally, **data processor** simply expresses what a computer *does* – it operates on digital data, and produces some actions as a result.

Types of computer

including: mainframe, mini-computer, microcomputer, Lisa, Macintosh, PC, Personal Computer, personal digital assistant (PDA), home computer, portable computer, palmtop computer, laptop computer, notebook computer, notepad, multimedia computer, super-computer

Newer computers tend to be smaller than those they replace. Names are needed to distinguish each new type of computer. Originally 'computer' meant something that filled a room, needed air-conditioning and several operators to run it. When the same level of computing power became available in a much smaller package, the rather ill-defined term *mini-computer* was introduced to describe the newcomer, while *mainframe* was reserved for the original monster.

The most significant development of the late 1970s was the introduction of a type of computer small enough and cheap enough to be bought by individuals. Apple Computers led the way commercially with their range of computers which evolved through the *Lisa*, offering the first convenient *graphical user interface* (see page 71), to the *Macintosh*. Later still, when IBM introduced the *Personal Computer* (or *PC*), a general name was needed for these types of computer. *Microcomputer* (or simply *micro*) became the general name, with 'PC' reserved for the IBM small business machines and *home computer* for the domestic hobbyist or games-playing machines.

Portable computers were the next development: *laptop computers* run off battery power and are suited for use while travelling, or at business meetings. Slightly smaller versions are called *notebook computers.*

A *palmtop computer* (sometimes called a *notepad*) is one that is very compact, and is designed to be carried in a pocket – because it is useful in situations where a mains-powered computer is not appropriate; most of these very small computers usually include software to transfer data to a PC or a larger machine. The current trend is for smaller and even more portable computers: the *personal digital assistant* (*PDA*) is a pocket-sized device without a keyboard (it is accessed through a pen-like stylus moving over the display, and the software recognises handwriting) but has failed to take the market by storm. The future in this area is extremely unpredictable.

A computer, often a PC, which has facilities for processing data as text, graphics, video moving images and sound, and can interface with a range of input and output devices for these different forms of data, is called a *multimedia computer.*

A *super-computer* is a very large machine which processes hundreds of millions of instructions per second. It is likely to have many parallel processors to achieve this. Data is processed simultaneously (in parallel) as well as sequentially to complete the tasks very quickly.

These names are all relative to one another, and are ill-defined: most personal computers now are more powerful than the earlier mainframes.

Analog computer

including: hybrid computer

Originally the word computer meant simply something that calculated (once, it even meant a *person* who performs calculations.). When modern computing began, as well as the digital computer described in the introduction, there were devices known as analog computers. Instead of operating on digital data, these used continuously variable quantities, such as voltages, or positions, to represent numbers, and combined these electrically or mechanically as a way of 'processing'. Some specialist applications still use analog computers. Inevitably, some computers, known as *hybrid computers* use both analog and digital technology in combination.

Computer

is an automatic, programmable, digital data processor. This definition is expanded and explained in the introduction to this section; the definition also excludes the *analog computer* (see above).

Computer generations

including: first, second, third, fourth and fifth generation computers, EDSAC, ENIAC, EDVAC, Atlas, Univac I, LEO (Lyons Electronic Office), ICL 1900, IBM 360

are a convenient way of distinguishing major advances in computer technology. The first three generations have well-accepted meanings, but the later generations tend to be used by manufacturers to stress the more modern features of a particular machine.

First generation computers were the earliest, and used valves, mercury delay lines, electrostatic memories and had very limited storage. Important first generation computers include the experimental **EDSAC**, **EDVAC** and **ENIAC** (which lacked stored-program facilities, and would now fail our definition of computer) and the production scientific computers **DEUCE** and **Pegasus**. Commercial machines were **LEO** (Lyons Electronic Office) and **Univac I**. These machines were all large, typically filling one or more rooms, and consumed large amounts of power.

Second generation computers arrived when the transistor replaced the valve as the basic component. They were consequently much more reliable, and consumed less power. They were cheaper, but still out of reach for most businesses and certainly for individuals. One of the most significant machines was *Atlas*.

Third generation computers saw the transistor replaced by the integrated circuit (the 'silicon chip'). They were again cheaper, and consumed less power and became even more reliable. One consequence of new design methods was the ability to produce whole families of similar, but differently-powered, computers – the ICL 1900 series, or the IBM 360 family, for example.

Fourth generation computers are those commonly encountered today. There is no single technological advance that distinguishes fourth generation computers from the third generation, except possibly the much greater use of large-scale integration of components on silicon chips, which resulted in increasing similarity of machine design. A dramatic fall in the cost of internal memory, and increases in the speed and capacity of external storage, led to new applications and new methods of programming. In addition there was a growing realisation that standardisation of software, particularly operating systems, is necessary.

Fifth generation computers are (still) something between an experimental prototype and an advertising agency's slogan. Many new computing concepts, that seemed to be significant advances on the previous generation, attracted this label: the use of formal mathematical logic in programming, for example, or the move away from 'traditional' computer architecture; increased use of distributed processing, parallel processing and so on. New methods of interacting with a computer – speech, touch – also came to be known as 'fifth generation'. The term should be used with caution, until the sixth generation arrives, and we fully understand what was in the fifth.

Computer system
including: configuration
is the complete collection of components (hardware, software, peripherals, power supplies, communications links) making up a single computer installation. The particular choice of components is known as the *configuration* – different systems may have the same configuration or not.

Front-end processor
is a computer dedicated to managing communications devices or other computers linked to a more powerful computer, generally a *mainframe* (see above). The front-end processor receives messages and commands from the communications devices, and organises these before passing them on to the larger computer for processing.

Hardware
is the physical part of a computer system – the processor(s), storage, input and output peripherals, etc. This is in contrast to the *software* (see 164) which includes application packages and the data in the storage.

Multiprocessor system
is a computer system with several *processors* (see below). These will work co-operatively, handling specific tasks (managing the screen display, doing arithmetic computation, handling peripherals) or simply sharing out the processing to enable parts of a task to proceed simultaneously (in parallel).

Network controller
is a computer dedicated to organising a computer network. It handles the communications between users and the shared resources, such as disks and printers. Some network topologies, such as the *star network* (see page 147), where the central computer is the network controller, can only operate with a controller; other arrangements may not use one. See also *server*, page 151.

Word processor
is a computer dedicated to, or primarily for, word processing. Some have displays which are the proportions of conventional paper sizes; some offer black text on a white, or coloured, background; most provide an extended keyboard with function keys for the software provided with the computer. Nearly all these facilities are now available as standard on general-purpose computers.

Central Processing Unit (CPU)
also known as: central processor, processor
including: microprocessor
is the main part of the computer. It performs all the internal processing activities in contrast to activities such as input and output, which are performed by *peripherals* (see *Peripherals*, Section B2, page 105). The central processing unit may include some memory. It is sometimes called the *central processor* or *processor*.

One special form of central processing unit is the *microprocessor* in which the components of the central processing unit are combined into a single unit. Microprocessors are used in microcomputers and computerised devices, for example the control circuits of washing machines.

B2   *Peripherals*

Peripherals are devices that can be attached to a computer system to do specialised jobs and which are frequently necessary for the effective use of a computer system. They are not necessarily provided as part of the computer. The range of devices is varied and many peripherals have been covered in other sections:

> *Additional memory, and terms relating to it, will be found in B3;*
>
> *Display devices and related terms will be found in B4;*
>
> *Printing devices and related terms will be found in B5;*
>
> *User interfaces often rely upon extra equipment being attached and details of such equipment will be found in A15;*
>
> *Sound, communications and control each have their own peripherals and details will be found in A11 (for sound), A4 and B7 (for communications) and A9 and B7 (for control).*

This section is concerned with those peripherals which do not find a place in the sections listed above.

There is a vast range of peripherals available but each performs one or both of the functions of **input** or **output**. At one time all memory, apart from immediate access memory, and all input and output devices were seen as 'peripheral'. This has changed, especially in microcomputer systems, and things that used to be seen as special input devices, such as a mouse, are now a fundamental part of the system.

Peripheral device
is the term used to describe an input, output, or backing storage device which can be connected to the central processing unit.

Input/Output device (I/O device)
is a peripheral unit which can be used both as an input device, or as an output device. In some instances, 'input/output device' may be two separate devices housed in the same cabinet.

Input device

is a peripheral unit that can accept data, presented in the appropriate machine-readable form, decode it and transmit it as electrical pulses to the central processing unit.

Document reader

is an input device that reads marks or characters made in predetermined positions on special forms.

Machine readable

including: mark sense reader, optical mark reader (OMR), optical character recognition (OCR), magnetic ink character recognition (MICR), bar code reader/scanner, wand

describes data that can be input to a computer without the need for any preparation. This may be a magnetic pattern stored on a credit card or travel ticket, or printing on paper which is also visible to humans. There is a variety of ways of reading printing into the computer, but in most cases there will be the need to have software to analyse what has been read in order to recognise it – for example, after a page of typed text has been read in using a *scanner* (see page 30), it requires complex processing before the image can be turned into codes for the individual characters.

A *mark sense reader* is an input device that reads special forms (or cards), by detecting the marks made in predetermined positions. The marks may be put on the form by hand or may be printed in some way.

An *Optical Mark Reader* (*OMR*) is an input device that reads marks made in predetermined positions on special forms (or cards) by a light-sensing method; for example, the numbers recorded on a National Lottery entry form.

Optical Character Recognition (*OCR*) is machine recognition of printed characters by light-sensing methods. For example, the reading of typed post codes when mail is automatically sorted or the machine-readable section of a European Community passport.

Magnetic Ink Character Recognition (*MICR*) is machine recognition of stylised characters printed in magnetic ink. The commonest application is the data printed on a bank (or building society) cheque: the cheque number, the branch number and the account number. These characters are both machine and human readable.

Bar code reader or *bar code scanner* is an input device used to read information in *bar code* form (see page 3). Sometimes the reader is built into equipment such as a supermarket checkout terminal, where it is usually referred to as a scanner. This form of reader shines laser light beams onto the object being scanned and interprets the patterns reflected by the bar code. An alternative form is a hand-held device, which is usually called a *wand*; this also works by sensing light reflected by the bar code.

Key-to-disk system
including: key-to-tape system
is an input device for accepting data from a keyboard and writing it straight onto magnetic disk. This method of data input for large computer systems has mostly been replaced by entry into microcomputers acting as terminals to the system or by automatic data capture systems, for example hand-held key-pads for meter readers. Where the data is written to tape it is called a *key-to-tape system*.

Output device
is a peripheral unit that translates signals from the computer into a human-readable form or into a form suitable for re-processing by the computer at a later stage.

Computer Output on Microfilm (COM)
is a technique for producing computer output directly on microfilm, for example the creation of computer-generated microfiches. This provides a very economical method of storing archive copies of documents and diagrams as well as making them generally available in microfiche form.

Original Equipment Manufacturer (OEM)
including: badging
is a firm which makes basic computer hardware for other manufacturers to build into their products. For example, a manufacturer using a microprocessor as a control device in a washing machine, or a computer manufacturer fitting another manufacturer's disk drive mechanisms into their computer. Many components of computer systems are made by only a small number of manufacturers, and are then built in to systems which are sold by other manufacturers under their own brand name: this practice is known as *badging*.

Plug compatible

including: plug and go

is used to describe any peripheral equipment, made by a manufacturer other than the computer maker, which is intended to be connected to the computer and will work successfully without any adaptation being needed. This has happened successfully only rarely in the past, and a group of hardware and software companies have co-operated to define a set of standards (known as *plug and go*) to make this more effective.

Timing information

including: index mark, clock mark, clock track

is required because mechanical devices cannot operate with the precision needed by computers. So, for example, an *index mark* in the form of an *index hole* (see page 114) is found on some floppy disks to provide a fixed reference point for reading and writing data. Another example is the *clock marks* making up the *clock track* which synchronise the reading of the items on a mark-sense document.

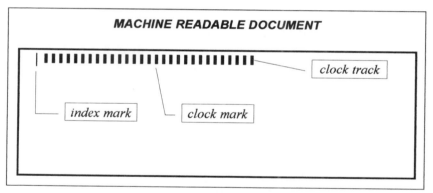

Figure B2.1: Clock track on a machine readable document

Operator's console

is the *terminal* (see page 150) used by the computer operator to control the operation of a mainframe or mini-computer.

B3   Memory

Memory is the name given to that part of a computer system in which data is held. This data is made up of files, either program files or data files. Computer memory serves two purposes. The first is to hold programs or data that the processor needs immediately; for this reason it is sometimes called **immediate access memory**. The second is to hold data that may be needed at some time; it is often called **backing store**. Immediate access memory must be able to be read (and be written to) very quickly, since most computer instructions require that data is moved around in the immediate access memory. Backup memory can have distinctly slower reading and writing times. Immediate access memory is usually about 1000 times as fast as backing store. The immediate access memory is located very close to the processor, so that signals take the shortest possible time in coming from and going to the processor; but backing store can be in separate units connected to the processor by cables.

Memory and storage have meanings that overlap and are often used as interchangeable words; but memory suggests data is immediately available whereas storage suggests that data has to be retrieved. Sometimes memory is described as **primary**, for the immediate access memory; **secondary**, for the principal backing store; and **auxiliary**, for other forms of backing store. A variety of other names are used for immediate access memory, such as IAS, main memory, the memory, the store; and for backing store, such as backup memory, peripheral memory, off-line storage.

Throughout the development of computers there has been a continual search for ways of improving memory technology. The search has been for reliable, compact storage devices with low energy consumption. Whenever a suitable new device has been developed, ways of cheap mass-production have been found.

Because of the different requirements for the two functions of memory, it is usual for completely different kinds of technology to be used in a particular computer system. For immediate access memory, most present-day computers use some form of random access memory integrated circuits, in which very large amounts of data can be stored in a single plastic encapsulated chip. For backing store, most use some form of magnetic storage, such as disks or tapes, and may also have read-only storage, such as CD-ROM.

Immediate access memory is sometimes in two parts. One part, called **cache** memory, is made up of a small capacity but exceedingly fast memory and is located next to the processor. The other part is much larger, and a copy of some of its contents is put into the cache memory in readiness for instant use. The choice of size for the main memory of a computer is partly determined by the addressing methods used and the cost of memory components. It is usual for computers to be sold with the potential for later memory expansion.

Backing store consists of the medium (the material on which the data is stored) and any associated mechanisms. Most computers use magnetic backing store (tapes or disks), while some use integrated circuit semiconductor memory, and optical systems are increasingly being used. As far as the user is concerned, the medium may be removable, for example tapes, floppy disks and optical disks; or fixed, for example hard disks. The advantage of using removable media is that an expensive mechanism can be used for a variety of purposes with cheap media. Fixed disks provide faster access and greater capacity than removable disks and are used to store programs and data that are frequently needed. Most computer systems now have both fixed and removable disks. A large computer system will have fixed disks, removable disks, tape storage and, possibly, optical storage. A personal computer will have at least a hard fixed disk and a floppy disk unit and, possibly, an optical disk unit.

Memory may be **volatile** or **permanent**. Volatile memory loses its data when there is no power supply to it, whereas permanent memory does not require power. All magnetic and optical media provide permanent memory as do some forms of integrated circuit memory. However the most widely used form of integrated circuit memory for immediate access store is volatile; this means that, when the computer is switched on, programs and data have to be loaded from backing store. If power is cut off, for some reason, then all data in memory will be lost.

Memory is often described by the type of *access* that is possible. For example, all the storage locations in immediate access memory can be directly accessed and the access time for all locations is the same; this is described as **random access memory**. In contrast, the data stored on a tape can only be reached by going through the tape, in sequence, until the right place is found; this is described as **serial access memory**. Storage on a disk is in concentric rings and is a collection of small sequential lengths of storage. Since disk storage can be so quickly accessed, it is generally thought of as direct (random) access storage.

Some forms of memory can only be read (**read-only**) and normally cannot be written to except during manufacture. Some semiconductor memory chips are manufactured as a blank memory array that can have data 'programmed' into it at a later time. One advantage is that some of these programmable memory chips can have the data erased and rewritten if necessary. Uses for programmable chips include storing programs for controlling traffic lights or lifts, and computer games programs. Most current optical disk technology is read-only, of which compact disk read-only memory (CD-ROM) is one example. Experience of technical advances suggests that it is only a matter of time before read-write optical devices become generally available at low cost. Some storage devices use a laser system to etch data onto a blank disk; the recorded data can then be read as often as needed but cannot be rewritten. They are called a write-once, read-many (WORM) devices.

Storage

also known as: memory
is a general term covering all units of computer equipment used to store data (and programs).

Store

also known as: memory
including: store location, address (store), main store, immediate access store (IAS), primary store, (memory) cell
The store, or memory, is the part of a computer system where data and instructions are held for use by the central processor and where the central processor puts results it generates. The computer store is made up of a large number of identifiable units, called *(store) locations*. Each store location has a unique label, called a *(store) address*, which is recognisable and used by the central processor. Those store locations that can be addressed directly by the central processor are called the *main store*, *immediate access store (IAS)* or *primary store*. A store location, sometimes called a *(memory) cell*, is capable of holding a single item of data, a *byte* (see page 124).

Backing store

also known as: secondary store, mass storage
including: magnetic disk storage, magnetic tape storage, optical disk storage, magneto-optical storage
is a means of storing large amounts of data outside the *immediate access store* (see above). A computer system will have at least one form of backing store. Most backing store uses magnetic storage, but increasing use is being made of optical storage systems. Backing store is sometimes referred to as *secondary store* or *mass storage.*

Magnetic disk storage is backing store in which flat rotatable circular plates, coated with a magnetic material, are used for storing digital data. The data is written to and read from a set of concentric circular *tracks* (see *magnetic disk*, below).

Magnetic tape storage is backing store which uses plastic tape coated on one
   side with magnetic material. Digital information is stored on the tape as a
   set of parallel *tracks* (see *magnetic tape*, below), which are written or
   read simultaneously.

Optical disk storage is backing store which uses plastic disks on which the
   data is stored as patterns on the surface. One method uses hollows etched
   into the surface of the disk for pre-recorded data in the form of
   CD-ROMs (see below). Other methods, such as *Phase Change Optical
   Disks* (see below) provide read/write optical storage.

Magneto-optical storage is backing store which uses plastic disks on which
   data is stored by a combination of optical and magnetic methods.

Cache memory

also known as: the cache
including: disk cache

is a part of the main store, between the central processor and the rest of the
main store. It has extremely fast access, so sections of a program and its
associated data are copied there to take advantage of its short fetch cycle. The
use of cache memory can greatly reduce processing time. It is sometimes
called the *cache.*

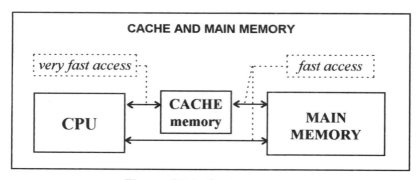

Figure B3.1: Cache memory

A way of speeding up the transfer of large amounts of data from disks is to
use a *disk cache,* which is a section of memory for holding data that has been
read from disk storage.

Disk drive

also known as: magnetic disk drive
including: fixed head disk unit, hard disk drive, Winchester drive, floppy disk drive, CD-ROM drive, CD-ROM jukebox
is the unit made up of the mechanism that rotates the disks between the *read/write heads* (see below), and the mechanism that controls the heads. Most disk drives have one set of read/write heads for each surface and have to be moved to the required track. A disk unit with one set of heads for each disk track is called a *fixed head disk unit*. This arrangement gives much faster access to data on the disk(s) but at increased cost.

Hard disk drives use rigid magnetic disk(s) enclosed in a sealed container. This has the advantage of allowing high recording density because the recording heads can be very close to the magnetic material on the disk. A small hard disk drive, sometimes known as a *Winchester disk (drive)*, is widely used in microcomputer systems as the principal back-up store in addition to one or more floppy disk drives.

Floppy disk drives use flexible disks which can be removed from their drives by the user, unlike hard disks which are permanently mounted. See *magnetic disk*, below.

CD-ROM drives (sometimes called a CD-ROM players) are very similar to audio compact disk players and read CD-ROM disks. A *CD-ROM jukebox* is a CD-ROM drive with a mechanism for automatically changing the current disk for another selected disk; it is similar to the old-fashioned jukebox for playing gramophone records.

Magnetic disk

also known as: computer disk, disk
including: hard disk, floppy disk, disk pack, exchangeable disk pack, diskette, index hole, track (disk), cylinder
is a circular disk, usually made of plastic, coated with a layer of magnetic material on which data can be stored by magnetically setting the arrangement of the magnetic material. This is done by electro-magnetic *read/write heads* (see below). Disks may have data stored on one side only (single sided) or on both sides (double sided). The disk may be rigid (a *hard disk*), or flexible (a *floppy disk*). Where a disk drive has multiple disks (a *disk pack*) these are generally rigid, hard disks, on a common spindle with read/write heads for each disk. If the disk pack is removable so that it can be exchanged for another complete pack, it is called an *exchangeable disk pack*.

A floppy disk (sometimes called a *diskette*) has to be protected by an outer covering which prevents the magnetic coating from being damaged and keeps out dirt. Floppy disks are made to agreed standard designs, which can be used on any drive for the same size of disk. The commonest size is 3½ inch, but the earlier 5¼ inch standard is still significantly used.

Floppy disks need to have some way of showing where the tracks start. In 5¼ inch disks this is done by an *index hole*. This is a small hole near the central hole, which lines up with a gap in the casing once every revolution. In 3½ inch disks, it is only possible to fit the disk onto the drive in one position. Floppy disks provide one of the most common ways of passing data and programs from one computer user to another.

The general layout of recording surfaces on a disk and on a multi-surface disk pack is shown in Figure B3.2.

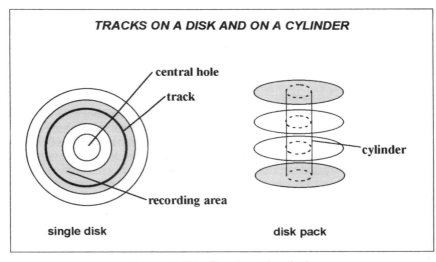

Figure B3.2: Track and cylinder

Data is stored on disks in concentric rings, called **tracks**. In a disk pack, a set of tracks one above the other, for example the tenth track on each disk, is called a **cylinder**. It is normal to store data which needs to be kept together, on a cylinder rather than on one disk, because the read/write heads will not need to move to access the data.

Disk format
including: sector, hard-sectored disk, soft-sectored disk, (disk) formatting, disk verification

is the arrangement and organisation of the *tracks* (see above) on a disk. Each track is divided into a number of equal-length portions, called *sectors* (see Figure B3.3). A sector is the smallest addressable portion of a track and is the smallest unit of data that is written to or read from a disk. Each sector on each track will hold the same amount of data, even though outer tracks are longer than inner tracks, so the *packing density* (see below) depends upon the distance of the track from the centre of the disk.

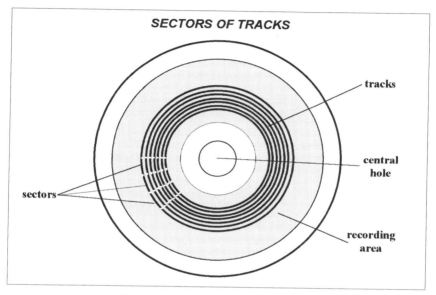

Figure B3.3: *Tracks and sectors*

If the sectors are partially or wholly created when the disk is made, the disk is called a ***hard-sectored disk***. If the sectors are created by software on an unformatted disk, the disk is called a ***soft-sectored disk.*** Floppy disks may be either hard- or soft-sectored.

The initial preparation of a blank disk for subsequent writing and reading by adding control information such as track and sector number is called ***(disk) formatting***. When a disk is formatted, it is also ***verified***; it is checked to ensure that all the tracks and sectors are fit for recording data. Formatting a disk that contains data will erase all the data on it. Floppy disks for personal computers need to be appropriately formatted for the machine on which they are to be used, although some machines may be able to read disks in a variety of formats. It is possible to buy floppy disks which are already formatted.

Disk array

including: RAID (Redundant Array of Inexpensive Disks)
is set of hard disk units used as if they are a single mass storage device. By using two disks to hold the same data, a disk drive fault will be unlikely to have any effect on the operation of the whole system. By writing some of the data to each of a number of disks, storage and retrieval of data can be speeded up. This method of organising backing store for large computer systems is known as *RAID*, which stands for *Redundant Array of Inexpensive* (or *Independent*) *Disks*. RAID systems provide a low-cost method of ensuring that losses of data are nearly impossible.

Read/write head

including: disk access time, seek time, latency, head crash, park
is the set of electro-magnets and necessary circuitry used to magnetise the magnetic material used for storage. Tape units have fixed heads and the tape moves past them. Most disk units have the set of heads on an arm which moves them from track to track, but fixed head disk units have a set of heads for each track, which greatly reduces the time taken to access data on the disk. Double-sided disks require a set of heads for each side. The time taken to get data from a disk, the *disk access time*, includes the time taken to move the heads to the correct track, called the *seek time*, and the time taken for the disk to rotate to the correct part of the track, sometimes called *latency*. However, some people use latency to mean the total waiting time.

Head crash is when the read/write heads hit the surface of a disk. This can cause serious damage to the mechanisms and loss of data. To avoid this happening with personal computers, for example when a machine is moved, the read/write heads are often automatically put in a safe position, *parked,* whenever they are not being used to access the disk. Following the proper procedures of closing all files before ending a session of work will ensure that the disk is properly parked. Some early personal computers require the user to give the command for parking the disk.

Magnetic tape drive

also known as: tape drive
is the mechanism that winds the tape between the spools across the read/write heads. Tape drives are capable of sensing the presence of stored data on the tape. Tape drives for cassettes are similar to those in domestic audio and video tape recorders.

Magnetic tape

including: (tape) spool, (tape) reel, (tape) cartridge, (tape) cassette, serial access storage, track (tape), frame, inter-block gap

is a storage medium consisting of a flexible plastic tape covered with magnetic material on one side, and kept on spools. The tape is similar to the tape used in domestic video systems, but of a higher quality since computer tapes need to be accelerated and decelerated very rapidly. The tape may be held on *reels* (or *spools*), requiring an operator to change the reels and thread the tape, or in *cartridges* or in *cassettes* (similar to the domestic video cassettes). This form of storage medium provides *serial access storage*. There are a number of methods of data storage on tape and a number of standard tape widths.

In older systems, many of which are still in use, the data is stored on the tape in parallel *tracks* using either a 7-track or a 9-track system on ½ - inch tape. A single character is represented by a line of magnetised spots, a *frame*, across the tape; these represent the bits for that character in an appropriate code.

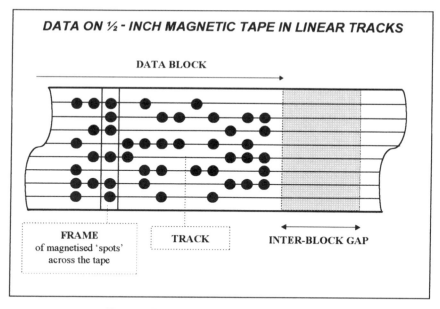

Figure B3.4: Magnetic tape (½ - inch)

Data is written to the tape in blocks, with a gap between each block, called an *inter-block gap*. The gap is needed for the tape to accelerate to the correct speed for reading or writing or to stop after reading or writing. Since the data is stored sequentially, finding an item of data will require that all the tape up to the data item is wound past the read/write heads until the required item is found. Figure B3.4 shows a diagrammatic representation of data on this form of magnetic tape; the data is stored as discrete areas of magnetism along each track.

More recent systems use the same technology as video recorders, where the data blocks are written on diagonal tracks (Figure B3.5) across the tape by a rotating head. This gives very high density and greater read/write speeds than the earlier tape systems.

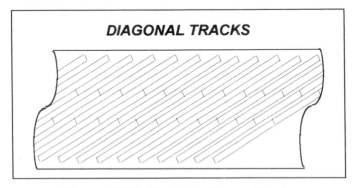

Figure B3.5: Blocks in diagonal tracks

Other tape formats include blocks arranged side by side on multiple tracks (Figure B3.6) and blocks one after another in a 'serpentine' arrangement with alternate tracks written in opposite directions (Figure B3.7).

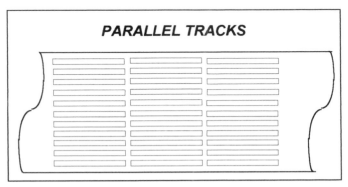

Figure B3.6: Blocks in parallel tracks

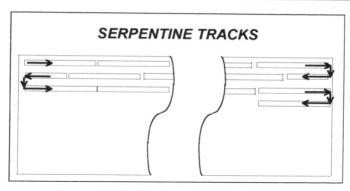

Figure B3.7: Blocks in serpentine tracks

Large amounts of data can be stored on a single tape. Tapes are used as backup or archive storage and are very useful for storing data which is required only on planned occasions, or when the majority of records will be accessed in any processing, for example, data which is updated monthly or quarterly. Applications which have very large storage requirements are increasingly using high packing density tapes for on-line purposes.

Tape streamer

is a small tape drive unit, usually using tape cassettes, with very large storage capacity. They are frequently used to make backup copies of data for security purposes.

Packing density

including: bits per inch (bpi), disk density, density
is a measure of the quantity of data that can be held per unit length of track on a storage medium. It is usually measured in **bits per inch** (**bpi**) and is the number of binary digits (or bits) stored in one inch (2.54cm) along each track.

Terms such as single density and double density (**DD**), quad density (**QD**) and high density (**HD**) are used to describe the packing density (or *density*) of magnetic disks (*disk density*). The interpretation of these terms is not uniform, since the size of the disk, the age of the drive and the sophistication of the operating system cause differences in meaning.

Semiconductor memory

also known as: integrated circuit memory
including MOS, CMOS
is a form of memory which uses integrated circuit semiconductor chips. The
storage capacity of this form of memory is very high, the time taken to read a
data item is very short and the access is direct. There are a number of
different forms of semiconductor storage, the more common ones use *MOS*
(*metal-oxide-semiconductor*) or *CMOS* (*complementary MOS*) technology.
The advantage of CMOS types is that they require little power to retain their
contents; powered by small batteries they can be used as *non-volatile memory*
while the computer is switched off. (See *volatile memory*, below.) Most
current computer designs use semiconductor memory for immediate access
storage.

RAM (Random Access Memory)

including: static RAM, dynamic RAM (DRAM), memory refresh
is memory that has the same access time for all locations. Each location holds
one *byte* (see page 124) and is directly addressable. RAM may be either
static, which holds its memory so long as there is a power supply, or *dynamic,*
which has to be *refreshed* by reading and rewriting the contents very
frequently (about every 2 milliseconds). Dynamic RAM (*DRAM*) is more
widely used than static RAM because it needs less power. Both dynamic and
static RAM are *volatile* (see *volatile memory*, below). See also
s*emiconductor memory,* above.

RAM disk

also known as: silicon disk
is memory which is addressed as if it were a very fast random access disk. It
behaves as an extremely fast backing store for the user but is usually volatile
and has to be loaded from backing store. It is normally an area of main
memory reserved for this use.

ROM (Read-Only Memory)

including: PROM (Programmable Read-Only Memory), EPROM (Erasable
PROM), EAROM (Electrically Alterable Read-Only Memory), EEPROM
(Electrically Erasable PROgrammable Memory), flash PROM, cartridge
is memory for which the contents may be read but cannot be written to by the
computer system. Read-only memory is used for both data and programs.
There are optical ROM systems (see *CD-ROM*, below), and semiconductor
(integrated circuit) ROM systems (see *semiconductor memory*, above).

The term **ROM** is frequently used to mean the (integrated circuit) read-only memory used to hold programs and associated data for building into computers. Software in ROM is fixed during manufacture, but there are other ways of putting programs and data into ROM.

PROM (*Programmable Read-Only Memory*) is a type of ROM which is manufactured as an empty storage array and is later permanently programmed by the user.

EPROM (*Erasable PROM*) is a type of PROM whose data can be erased by a special process (for example, by exposure to ultraviolet radiation) so new data can be written as if it were a new PROM.

EAROM (*Electrically Alterable Read-Only Memory*) and *EEPROM* (*Electrically Erasable Programmable Read-Only Memory*), sometimes called *flash PROM*, are other similar types of read-only memory.

Some small computers and games computers use software on (integrated circuit) ROM which is packaged in plug-in modules called *cartridges.* This is a convenient way of preventing the software from being copied.

Content-addressable storage
also known as: associative storage
is a physically separate module of storage, designed to allow access to a location by its contents rather than by an address label. The normal address decoder logic is replaced by logic which compares the contents of part of each store with the address item. The remainder of each store contains indications of where the required data is stored.

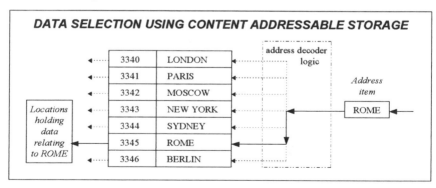

Figure B3.8: Content-addressable storage

Optical storage

including: CD-ROM (Compact Disk Read-Only Memory), videodisk, laser disk, EB disk (Electronic Book disk), WORM (Write-Once, Read-Many), multisession CD, Photo-CD, Magneto-Optical Disk, Phase Change Optical Disk

uses laser technology to etch the surface of a storage medium to form minute patterns which represent the data. The scattering effect on a narrow laser beam is used to read the data which may be digital or analog. At present, the process of making optical disks requires costly equipment, but this may change. The digital technology is the same as that used in audio compact disks (CDs).

CD-ROM (*Compact Disk Read-Only Memory*), which uses the same size of disk as audio CDs, is a read-only form of backing store used to hold large amounts of data. CD-ROM disks are pressed from a master disk in the same way that audio CDs are made. A *videodisk*, sometimes called a *laser disk*, is an equivalent analog form, which uses large disks like long playing gramophone records, for which the domestic equipment is quite rare. A recent development is the *EB disk* (*Electronic Book disk*), which uses a 3 inch disk. The data on CD-ROM may include programs as well as sound, graphics or text data. CD-ROM with a computer capable of manipulating, storing and outputting high quality sound and graphics is a multimedia system. See *multimedia computer*, page 101.

WORM (*Write-Once, Read-Many*) is an optical (compact) disk system, which allows the user to write data on the next available portion of the disk. A portion of the disk can only have data written on it once, but this data can be read as often as required. Some worms allow the overwriting of data so as to spoil or erase it. *Multisession-CD*, which is designed to capture and store materials created during separate work sessions, is one example of a worm; another form is *Photo-CD*, which stores conventional camera images on optical disk.

Magneto-Optical Disk is a re-writable optical disk which uses magnetic and optical techniques. Writing uses a laser beam to heat a small part of the surface of the disk and, at the same time, a magnetic field arranges the magnetic material in this heated area in one of two ways. Reading uses the effect that the magnetic field on the surface of the disk has on a weak laser beam.

Phase Change Optical Disk is a re-writable optical disk which uses a laser to read and write data. It uses three strengths of laser signal. The weakest signal is used to read data; the other two signals are used to write data, by making parts of the material of the disk surface reflective or non-reflective to the weakest signal.

Block

including: bucket

is the name for the smallest unit of data which is transferred between backing store and main store in one operation. In large computer systems, a *bucket* defines a unit of storage in random access memory. A bucket will contain a (variable) number of blocks. Access to the data is by reference to the bucket it is in.

Memory map

including: disk map, file allocation table (FAT)

describes the way storage is organised in a computer. For example, sections of memory may be allocated to the screen display, program code, variables. The memory map for disk storage is called a *disk map.* It describes how the information held on the disk is organised, and is kept on the disk. It may be held as a *bit map* (see page 32). Details of where files are stored in backing store is kept in a *file allocation table* (*FAT*), which is a file kept on the backing store. See also *directory*, page 82.

Scratch pad

also called: work(ing) store

including: scratch file, scrap file, work(ing) file, scratch tape

is a section of immediate access store reserved as a temporary working area for use by an application. It is also called a *work store* or *working store*. An area of file space on backing store assigned for this purpose is called a *scratch file, scrap file, work file* or *working file.* If tape is used, it is called a *scratch tape*. See also *clipboard*, page 8.

Virtual storage

also known as: virtual memory

is a means of apparently extending main storage, by allowing the programmer to access backing storage in the same way as immediate access store. Often personal computers provide this facility, using an area of disk as if it were main memory, without the user being aware of it. This has an advantage when running large programs but the processing speed will be slow.

Volatile memory

including: non-volatile memory, permanent memory

is a form of storage which holds data only while power is supplied. This is in contrast to **non-volatile memory**, which keeps its contents even when the system is switched off. All currently used forms of magnetic storage and optical disk storage are non-volatile, but most other forms of storage are volatile. **Permanent memory** retains its contents regardless of power supply and cannot be erased or altered; many forms of read-only memory (ROM) are permanent.

Write protection

including: blocking ring, write-inhibit ring, write-permit ring, request verification

is the prevention of unintentionally overwriting data on backing store. This can be achieved either by hardware features or by provisions in software.

Hardware write protection is built into floppy disk drives and floppy disk cases; for the older, 5¼ inch disks a cut-away portion of the case has to be covered over with an adhesive patch, while for 3½ inch disks there is a sliding cover for a hole in the case. There are no similar standards for large disk units; each manufacturer provides their own system. There is no hardware write protection for small hard disks in personal computers. Tape units have removable **blocking rings** behind the tape spools which act either as **write-inhibit** or as **write-permit rings** depending on the system used; cassettes or cartridges have sliding tabs.

Software methods include double checking a request (**request verification**) if it will over-write or delete a file, checking the characteristics of file names to see if they are protected and asking for passwords before overwriting or deleting any data.

Bit (BInary digiT)

including: least significant bit (LSB), most significant bit (MSB)

is a single digit from a binary number, it is either a 0 or a 1. It is the smallest unit of storage since all data is stored as binary codes.

The **least significant bit** (**LSB**) is the bit in a binary number with the least place value and the **most significant bit** (**MSB**) is the bit in a binary number with the greatest place value.

Byte

is a group of bits, typically 8, representing a single character. This is normally the smallest grouping used by a computer. A byte may also be used to represent a small number.

B4　　Display Devices

Human beings possess a very high resolution, multicolour and fast-moving vision system. Thus it is understandable why so much technical effort has gone into producing displays from computer systems that can exploit the facilities of the human eye.

Much of the current display technology uses the cathode ray (television) tube. The tube looks like a large electric light bulb with a flat end. The user only sees the flat end. The electronics of the system makes the end glow with patterns of dots. It is the number and nature of these dots that determines the quality of the picture that the user sees.

For such applications as word processing then perhaps a monochrome (one colour) display is all that is needed but at the present state of development the software that would be used to produce the word processed document would no doubt require a colour display. We are now at the stage where colour display is considered to be the norm.

All the colours of the rainbow can be made by mixing various amounts of red, green and blue light. A colour display screen is coated with substances that glow when they are hit by electric particles (electrons).

The coating is arranged in horizontal lines of **triads**. A triad is a cluster of three dots that will glow; one will glow red, one green and one blue. The electronics of the whole system will excite different members of the triad to a greater or lesser amount, so as to produce a glowing dot (a **pixel**) of the required colour and brightness. It is an arrangement of a large number of these pixels that produces the final picture. The screen picture needs to be able to change quickly, anything from just simple text editing to a fast-moving graphics image. This ability to change is achieved because the picture is redrawn many times a second (in the range of 25 to 72 times) even if it is not actually changing. This screen **refresh** process is done by the electron beam making a horizontal sweep over each line of triads. It is technically easier, and thus cheaper, for the screen refresh to be done in two passes; every other line of triads is refreshed on a first pass, then the other lines are refreshed at the second pass; this is called **interlace** scanning. Interlace scanning is the method normally used in domestic television but a system that refreshes all the lines of triads in sequence, called **non-interlaced** scanning, is used in a number of designs for computer display screens.

The electronics that pass the information from the computer to the screen device are generally specific to the type of screen device. These electronics have to be installed by fitting a specific electronics board, called a **display**

adapter, into the computer. For example, when a system has a VGA display this means a VGA screen device and a matching VGA display adapter in the computer.

The development of laptop computers has required high-performance flat-screen display systems. This has been achieved by major enhancements to liquid crystal technology, which was originally developed for pocket calculators. In its basic form, liquid crystal display consists of a thin layer, a film, of fluid sandwiched between two sheets of glass or plastic. Complex wiring is used to apply voltages to different small areas of the film of liquid. The applied voltage alters the ability of the liquid to reflect or transmit light. Thus a pixel display is built up of light and dark dots of varying intensity. One way of producing colour is to have three layers of different types of liquid, with different colour characteristics, where each layer has its own associated wiring. Some systems rely on reflected light and cannot be used in poor lighting conditions. Back lighting systems, where the liquid films transmit light from a light source behind the screen, give a more easily viewed display than reflective systems.

Monitor
including: monochrome monitor, colour monitor, scan rate, multiscan monitor
is the term generally used for any device that displays information using a cathode ray tube. Although this definition could include a standard television set, a monitor normally does not have the receiving part of a television set. All monitor displays are made up of illuminated dots on the screen. Monitors may be monochrome or colour.

Monochrome monitors give a display of varying intensity of a single colour, for example white, green or orange on a dark (black) background.
Colour monitors give a display with a range of colours determined by the colour circuitry in the monitor and the computer.

Monitors may have a fixed or variable *scan rate*, that is how often the image is redrawn or refreshed (see *screen refresh*, below). Monitors that can operate at different scan rates are called *multiscan monitors* or *multisync monitors*; they can adjust to different scan rates set by a *video adapter* (see below). Multiscan monitors first appeared in 1985 and are essential for modern high definition display systems, such as *SVGA* and *EGA* (see below).

Video adapter

also known as: display adapter, graphics adapter

is the circuitry which generates the signals needed for a video output device to display computer data. The data may be text only or text and graphics. The circuits are contained on a circuit board which is installed in the computer with output via a cable to the display unit (the monitor). A variety of adapters have been devised and sold. Most are associated with one computer manufacturer and require the use of a particular design of *monitor* (see above). There is a range of *standard adapters for IBM PCs* (and IBM compatibles), some of which are described in Table B4.1 (page 130). In addition, there are video adapters from other manufacturers which can be installed in PCs. Computers which are not IBM compatible frequently use their own video adapters with different standards.

Frame

including: interlace

is used to describe a screenful of information treated as a single unit. An example is a response frame for the input of data in a screen input data capture system.

In electronics, a frame is one complete screen picture. In a standard television set, this consists of 625 separate lines; a new frame is transmitted every 1/25 of a second, as two *interlaced* fields: the first field is the odd-numbered lines and the second is the even-numbered lines.

PAL (Phase Alternating Line)

is the UK standard method of encoding colour information in a television signal. If a domestic television set is used as a display device via the ordinary aerial socket, the computer must contain a PAL encoder for colour.

Palette

is the range of display colours available in the computer system. Any particular display system may not be able to support the total number of colours, hence a selection is made from the possible palette. The user may be allowed to change this selection.

Pixel

is a contraction of 'picture-element'. As used in graphics, it is the smallest element of a display. A pixel will have one or more attributes of colour, intensity (or brightness) and flashing.

Pixel graphics

is where a picture is constructed of a rectangular array of dots. Each dot may be any of the colours available to the computer but it is not possible for a dot to be split into smaller pieces. This means that it is impossible to have detail smaller than the size of the *pixels* (see above).

Raster graphics

including: raster, scan, interlaced scan, non-interlaced scan, scan frequency, screen resolution, dot pitch, low-resolution graphics, High-Resolution Graphics (HRG)

is a method of producing an image on a display screen. The image is drawn on a cathode ray tube (a CRT) by illuminating *pixels* (see above) as horizontal lines of dots covering the whole screen, this is called the *raster*. An electron beam sweeps over these lines of pixels, drawing the display many times a second, in the same way that a picture is drawn on a television set (see *frame*, above).

Sweeping over the lines of the raster display is called *scanning*. The scan may be done by drawing alternate lines (line 1 followed by line 3, and so on) on a first pass and then the rest of the lines on a second pass. This is called an *interlaced scan*, and is the method used in television sets. Alternatively the scan may draw each line successively (line 1 followed by line 2, and so on), called a *non-interlaced scan*. How often the screen is scanned is called the *scan frequency*.

The quality of a raster display depends upon the *screen resolution*, which is usually quoted as the number of pixels in a row × the number of rows (horizontal × vertical), and the *dot pitch*, which is the size of a dot (pixel) on the screen. Values of between 0.28mm and 0.38mm for the dot pitch are considered acceptable; this is between 100 and 70 dots per inch. To provide an acceptable image on a large screen, the pixel resolution has to be increased to give the same dot pitch as on a smaller screen. In general, raster graphics will produce untidy display of any line which is neither vertical nor horizontal. If high-quality screen display of line drawings is required, then *vector graphics* (see below) is the appropriate system.

A number of general descriptions of display resolution are used:

Low-resolution graphics is generally applied to graphical display units where simple pictures can be built up by plotting large blocks of colour or by using special graphics characters. It is used for *teletext* images (see page 23).

High-Resolution Graphics (HRG) is generally applied to graphical display units capable of plotting around 300 or more pixels in the width of a *monitor* screen (see above).

Graphical Display Unit (GDU)

is an output device, incorporating a cathode ray tube (CRT), on which both line drawings and text can be displayed. The term has become used for display systems specifically for high-quality graphics work. A graphical display unit is often used in conjunction with a light-pen to input or re-position data. High-quality graphical display units normally use *vector graphics* (see below).

Vector graphics

is a screen display method using a cathode ray tube (CRT) in which each line of a drawing is drawn on the screen individually. A line can be drawn in any direction (although there is a minimum width of a line) and so the display is a more accurate presentation of the picture with no jagged edges. The resolution of vector graphics screens is usually very high so that the size of pixels is small, which gives the high-quality display. Vector graphics is an expensive technique to implement with the result that most displays use *raster graphics* (see above). See also *drawing package*, page 31 and *painting package*, page 32.

Font

is the set of printing or display characters in a particular type, style and size. The characters may take the form of pictures.

Liquid Crystal Display (LCD)

is a display technique that uses the phenomenon that certain liquids alter their ability to reflect or transmit light if a voltage is applied to them. Originally used for pocket calculators it is now common for laptop computers.

Light Emitting Diode (LED)

is a display that uses the property of some semiconductor diodes to emit light when a voltage is applied to them. Their power consumption is negligible and they give off no heat. They are commonly used as indicator lights on devices such as disk drives. They are also useful for monitoring the logic state of lines in control applications.

RGB (Red Green Blue)

describes a method of connecting a computer to a (colour) display monitor in which the colour information is transmitted as three separate signals. RGB signals do not need to be decoded, as does a *PAL* signal (see above). Thus, definition is generally better using an RGB connection.

IBM PC-COMPATIBLE VIDEO GRAPHICS ADAPTERS

NAME	DESCRIPTION	RESOLUTION	character size	COLOUR PROVISION
		text: (rows × characters) graphics: (pixels: width × height)		
Monochrome Display Adapter (MDA) Released 1981	text but no graphics: (for monochrome monitors)	text: 25 rows of 80 characters graphics: not available		monochrome only
Hercules graphics adapter Released 1982	text and graphics (for monochrome monitors)	text: 32 rows of 80 characters graphics: 720 × 320 pixels	10×9	monochrome only
Colour Graphics Adapter (CGA) Released 1981	colour text **two** colour graphics modes: (MDA compatible)	text: 25 rows of 80 characters graphics: 640 × 200 pixels graphics: 320 × 200 pixels	8×8	16 foreground + 8 background two colours four colours
Enhanced Graphics Adapter (EGA) Released 1984	improved version of CGA text and graphics bit mapped	graphics: 640 × 350 pixels		16 colours
Video Graphics Array (VGA) Released 1987	improved version of EGA text and graphics bit mapped	graphics: 640 × 480 pixels		256 colours

| Super Video Graphics Array (SVGA) Released 1988 | Analog display system: needs multiscan monitor | graphics: 800 × 600 pixels | 16 colours infinite range of shades of grey |
| Extended Graphics Array (XGA) Released 1991 | Analog display system: needs multiscan monitor | graphics: 1024 × 768 pixels | 256 colour text theoretically infinite range of colours; in practice usually limited to 262,144 ($= 2^{18}$) |

Notes:

The quality of screen image depends upon the screen **dot pitch** rather than just on the numbers of pixels. On a 14-inch screen with 1024 × 768 pixels the dot pitch is 0.28mm (approx. 90 dots/inch); to achieve similar quality of image on a 17-inch screen requires a resolution of 1280 × 1024 pixels (dot pitch 0.26mm, approx. 98 dots/inch).

The vertical and horizontal resolutions are not the same for all the above specifications.

The above specifications were all promoted by IBM. After 1991, a number of other manufacturers developed adapters with different screen proportions and higher resolutions such as 1280 × 1024 pixels.

See also *pixel* and *monitor* (above) and *bit map* (page 32).

Table B4.1: Graphics adapters

Screen refresh
including: refresh rate, Vertical Refresh Rate (VRR)
is the process of continuously energising the glowing substances on a cathode ray tube device to keep the display visible. The screen is refreshed between 25 to 72 times per second (known as the ***refresh rate***) depending on the display system used. The technique allows the easy display of changing images.

Vertical Refresh Rate (VRR) is related to the horizontal sweeps that the electron beam makes in a cathode ray tube (CRT) display. Once an image has been entirely repainted by horizontal sweeps then it has been vertically refreshed. A low vertical refresh rate tends to produce flicker. A *VGA* monitor has a vertical refresh rate of 60 - 70 scans per second and the standard for *SVGA* monitors is 72 scans per second. See also the table of *video graphics adapters for IBM PCs*, Table B4.1, page 130.

Video RAM (VRAM)
is a separate high-speed memory into which the processor writes the screen data, which is then read to the screen for display. This avoids the use of any main memory to hold screen data.

Video data compression
including: delta compression, JPEG, MPEG
is the use of electronic methods to reduce the amount of data that has to be included when video data, either for still or moving pictures, is stored or transmitted. For moving pictures (video), the principles involve identifying those parts of the picture which change from one scan to the next, and sending data only about the changes, which is known as ***delta compression***. This alone will save a significant amount of transmission and storage capacity. Periodically a complete new whole picture will need to be sent.

The Joint Photographic Expert Group (***JPEG***) has defined standards for still picture compression, and this format for storage or transmission is called JPEG. These standards have been extended by the Motion Picture Expert Group (***MPEG***) to cover moving images. MPEG provides a method of video data compression in common use for storing and transmitting films.

B5   *Printers*

A printer is connected to a computer for the single purpose of transferring the information from the computer to paper. The version printed out on paper is often referred to as hard copy. There are many types of printer that can be connected to a computer system varying in quality, cost and use. Broadly speaking the printers divide themselves up into three groups: **character printers, dot matrix and ink jet printers** and **laser printers**.

   Character printers, which print a single character at a time, were really a development from typewriters, often with all the characters on a single element (a golf-ball or a daisy-wheel). They were mechanical in action and, as a result, printed slowly and tended to be extremely noisy. However, they produced good quality printing and so were often used by businesses. Today they are hardly used as there are now other printers that can work faster, produce quality printing, do it quietly and are more flexible.

   Dot matrix printers rely upon a print head moving in straight lines across the paper. Inside the print head is a vertical line of pins each of which can print a dot on the paper. By making the pins hit the paper at the right moment it is possible to print a pattern of dots that looks like any character that is wanted. For example:

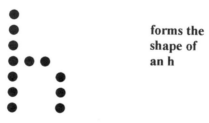

**forms the
shape of
an h**

   The advantage of the dot matrix printer is that it is possible to produce any character or shape that is required simply by arranging for the appropriate pins to be 'fired' at the right moment - this makes it useful for printing out a copy of a piece of computer graphics (i.e. some form of picture or design). It can also be made to produce effects such as different styles of letter, different sizes of letter and even produce output resembling a document produced by a publisher. Other advantages are that such printers are relatively cheap, they will work with almost any quality of paper and some of them can even print in colour by using a special ribbon containing the four colours black, red, blue and yellow. They are generally able to print on either continuous paper or single sheets.

Ink jet printers (sometimes called *bubble jet*) create the printed image by forcing droplets of ink from a cartridge through a fine nozzle onto the paper, forming the characters by patterns of ink droplets similar to a dot matrix printer. The print quality of most ink jet printers is much better than dot matrix printers, however they do suffer the problem of saturating the paper with ink, which causes the paper to crinkle —special paper for ink jet printers removes this problem, but at a cost. It is possible to print in colour with them, the better printers having four separate cartridges for cyan, magenta, yellow and black (sometimes referred to as CMYK, the K standing for Key or black). These printers have the advantages of being compact, many of them are classed as portable, and they produce print quality rivalling that produced by a laser printer (but not as quickly).

Laser printers essentially use the Xerographic technology of the modern photocopier. An image is produced on a special drum that then attracts the toner (a black fine plastic powder) where the lines/areas of the image are, the paper then presses against the drum transferring the toner image to the paper. The paper then goes through a heater which melts the toner onto the paper before it emerges from the machine. The only difference between a laser printer and a photocopier is in the way the image is formed on the drum. A printer uses a laser light source to write the image onto the drum from the image in the printer's memory. This requires that a laser has to have a fairly large amount of memory in order to print a page — at least 1 Mb, but preferably more. Colour laser printers do exist, but they are very, very expensive.

The main advantages of a laser printer over almost any other printer are:
    i) the quality of printing (though this does vary from one machine to another)
    ii) the speed of printing (from about 4 pages per minute up to 16 pages per minute for small machines)

The main disadvantages of a laser printer are:
    i) can only print complete pages as opposed to individual lines
    ii) the size of the machine
    iii) the relatively high running costs (toner cartridges, paper, etc)

In summary, deciding upon a printer is not easy as all printers today can print anything that your computer can produce. Probably cost and quality of print are the two main areas to focus upon - and noise, if you are likely to be printing a lot or late at night.

Printer

including: print head

is an output device producing characters or graphic symbols on paper. There are many methods of printing and of organising the operation of a printer. Many forms of smaller printers use a moving *print head* which travels backwards and forwards across the paper and carries the printing mechanism. For a summary of information about printers see *PRINTERS Types and Characteristics*, Table B5.1, page 140.

Character printer

including: daisy wheel printer, golf ball printer, bi-directional printer, logic-seeking

is one which prints the characters one at a time.

A *daisy wheel printer* is a character printer where the characters are arranged near the ends of the spokes on a rimless wheel (like the petals of a daisy), the wheel turning to give the character. A hammer is used to strike the character petal onto a ribbon against the paper. The daisy wheel is manually interchangeable to enable alternative character sets to be used.

A *golf ball printer* is a character printer using a moving spherical print head as in many electric typewriters. The golf ball twists to set the character and then strikes a ribbon against the paper. The head is easily removable enabling many different character sets to be used.

Both daisy wheel and golf ball printers have a moving print head, which holds the daisy wheel or golf ball and their mechanisms, and can travel from side to side across the paper.

A *bi-directional printer* is a character printer where the right-to-left return movement of the print head is used to print a second line, thus increasing printing speed.

Logic-seeking is the ability of a character printer to organise its own operation to cope efficiently with blank, short or right-justified lines. Such a printer does not always alternate its direction of printing.

Impact printer

is a term applied to any printer which creates marks on the page by striking an inked ribbon (or carbon paper) against the page. The object that strikes the ribbon may form complete characters at one strike, as in a typewriter, or may form a pattern of dots, as in a pin dot matrix printer.

Dot matrix printer

including: pin printer, thermal printer

is a printer which forms characters or graphics images out of ink dots in a rectangular matrix of printing positions. The image is made up of dots in the same sort of way that a screen image is generated using *pixel graphics* (see page 128).

The term is frequently used for ***pin printers***, which were the first kind of printer to build up characters by printing patterns of dots. The dots are printed by pins striking a ribbon against the paper. A vertical line of pins is mounted in a print head which travels backwards and forwards across the paper.

A ***thermal printer*** uses wires arranged like the pins of a dot matrix printer which are heated to form dots on heat-sensitive paper. Thermal printers are very quiet but do not produce good quality printing.

Ink jet printer

also known as: bubble jet printer
including: CMYK, ink cartridge, print cartridge

is one which uses a fine jet of quick-drying ink to produce the printing. What is printed may be text or graphics. A monochrome ink jet printer will print characters in black and diagrams in shades of grey. Colour versions use four colours, cyan, magenta, yellow and black (sometimes referred to as *CMYK*, the K standing for Key or black). The ink is held in small containers, called ***ink cartridges*** or ***print cartridges,*** from which the ink is directly jetted onto the paper. These cartridges are mounted in a print head which travels backwards and forwards across the paper.

Page printer

is one which forms and prints a whole page in one operation, for example a *laser printer* (see below).

Laser printer

is a page printer which uses a laser to 'write' the image to be printed onto a light-sensitive drum. The drum then uses electrostatics (as in a photocopier) to attract toner, a black fine plastic powder, to coat the image with powder. Paper is then pressed against the drum transferring the toner to the paper. The paper is then heated to melt the toner onto the paper.

Line printer

including: barrel printer, print hammer, chain printer

is one that prints a complete line of characters at one time, and hence is generally faster than a character printer. The printers described below are large machines capable of printing at very high speeds and are generally only used with mainframe computers.

In a *barrel printer* the complete character set is provided at each printing position, embossed on the surface of a horizontal barrel or cylinder, and each printing position has a *print hammer*, which is used to press the paper against a ribbon to print a character. The barrel turns and as the correct character for a position occurs, its print hammer strikes the paper against a ribbon and onto the character, causing the character to be printed.

In a *chain printer* the characters are carried on a continuous chain between a set of print hammers and the paper. The chain moves along the print line and as the required character appears at a print position the print hammer strikes the paper against a ribbon and onto the character.

Unless these printers are well maintained the quality can be poor with the characters badly aligned.

Font

including: printer driver, font cartridge

is the set of printing or display characters in a particular type, style and size. Printers may offer a choice of fonts, either by exchanging the printer head (daisy wheel or golf ball) or by software control as with dot matrix, ink jet or laser printers. The font options, which can be selected by the user, may be stored in the computer and accessed through *printer drivers*, which are part of the system software that formats data for printing, or stored in read only memory (ROM) *font cartridges* installed in the printer.

Page description language

including: Postscript

is a kind of computer language used to pass instructions to printers for setting up the data to be printed.

Postscript is a page description language used by some laser printers. The computer would code its printout requirements, for example the size, direction and style of a piece of text or the format for a diagram. These would then be interpreted by the postscript translator, which is in the printer, into the corresponding image of dots ready for printing.

Print quality

including: correspondence (or letter) quality, Near Letter Quality (NLQ), draft quality

is a description of how well formed the characters are when printed. The descriptions are in terms of the standards expected of printed output for different purposes.

Correspondence quality, also known as *letter quality,* is the quality of print obtained from daisy wheel printers, which is similar to the quality of a traditional typewriter, or from ink jet and laser printers.

Near Letter Quality (NLQ) is the best available quality on a dot matrix printer, which used to be considered acceptable for correspondence, but with the availability of low-cost ink jet printers few people now find this good enough.

Draft quality is a quality of printing whose characters are not well shaped, but can be printed quickly. Often this is the standard print available from dot matrix printers.

Graph plotter

also known as: plotter

including: flat-bed plotter, digital plotter, incremental plotter

is an output device which draws lines on paper by moving a pen in a holder relative to the paper on which the drawing is being made. In some designs the paper is on a roller and both the pen and the roller move; in others the paper is fixed on a flat surface, a *flat-bed plotter*, and all the movements are made by the pen.

A *digital plotter* receives digital input specifying the co-ordinates of the points to be plotted, together with information about how the point to be plotted is joined to the current point.

An *incremental plotter* receives input data specifying increments to its current position, rather than data specifying co-ordinates.

Paper feed mechanism

including: friction feed, tractor feed, (cut) sheet feeder

is the means of making the paper move through the printing process. Many printers require that the paper is moved after a line (or sometimes half a line) has been printed.

Friction feed is a mechanism for advancing paper by gripping it between rollers.

Tractor feed is a mechanism for advancing paper by the use of perforations down the side of the paper and a toothed wheel (a sprocket).

Cut sheet feeder (also known as *sheet feeder*) allows ordinary separate sheets of paper to be automatically fed in for printing. Where a sheet feeder is not provided as part of the printer, it may be available as an accessory.

Media
is the collective name for materials (tape, disk, paper, cards, etc.) used to hold data.

Hard copy
also known as: printout
is computer output printed on paper.

Continuous stationery
including: fan-fold paper, multipart stationery
is printer paper which is perforated to make pages and folded in alternate directions at each set of perforations to form a stack, *fan-fold paper*. It normally has a tear-off margin on both sides with holes for a tractor feed mechanism to use. It can be a series of pre-printed forms. For some applications the stationery may consist of several sheets together (termed *multipart stationery*) either with carbon paper in between or made of pressure-sensitive paper, so that several copies are printed at the same time using an impact printer. See also *pre-printed stationery*, below.

Pre-printed stationery
has certain fixed information already printed on each sheet so that the computer can fill in the gaps. This increases the speed of printing and improves the presentation. The paper may be cut sheets or continuous stationery. Common examples are customer accounts for gas and electricity, and computer printed cheques.

Bursting
is the separating of *continuous stationery* (see above) into individual sheets by tearing the paper along the perforations.

Decollate
is to separate the sheets of *multipart continuous stationery* (see above) which has been produced as output from a printer.

PRINTER TYPES AND CHARACTERISTICS

CHARACTER PRINTERS	MATRIX PRINTER	PAGE PRINTER
line printers (barrel, chain), golf ball, daisy wheel	*pin dot matrix printers, ink jet printers*	*laser printers*
impact on a ribbon or carbon paper is used to form the characters	use *pins* (impact or thermal) or *ink jet* to print the image	use photocopier principles
print individual characters, text only	can print text and graphics	can print text and graphics
characters are printed as complete characters in a single action	text and images made up of dots in a matrix pattern (similar to a screen image)	print a complete page at a time
line printers etc. – poor print quality; *daisy wheel* etc. – very good print quality	print quality depends on the resolution (dots per inch)	capable of very high resolution
usually only a single (limited) font available at a time	wide range of fonts available through software	wide range of fonts available through software
restricted line spacing, (often only full lines)	flexible line spacing	can print anywhere on the page print area (possibly excluding margins)
unlimited page length, fixed maximum width	unlimited page length, fixed maximum width	fixed maximum page length and width
can print multi-part stationery	*pin printers* – can print multi-part stationery; *ink jet printers* – cannot print multi-part stationery	cannot print conventional multi-part stationery
usually only single colour, fixed intensity	can print in colour, *ink jet* can print a range of shades	can print colour, can print a range of shades
line printers can print at high speeds	slow to medium speed printing	can print at high speeds

Obsolescent technology but some **line printers** are still in use in large-scale data processing contexts	Replacement for typewriter-style printers: generally compact machines: wide range of speeds and quality.	Have almost completely replaced the older **line printers** for large volume printing. Sizes range from desk-top to very large, floor standing machines.
Line printers use a print hammer for each print position to strike the paper and ribbon/carbon paper against embossed type on barrels or chain loops when the right character is in position: daisy wheel and golf ball printers print a character and then move to the next print position and have easily changeable fonts.	Print mechanisms move backwards and forwards over the paper, which advances after each pass by the print mechanism. Print quality is determined by the number of pins or ink bubble size and the minimum size of head and paper movements.	Image of the page is 'written' by lasers onto a special drum as an electrostatic charge: the drum attracts toner particles which are transferred to the page and heated to set the image.
Application range: small office machines to large-scale data processing	Application range: personal printers to network printers on small networks	Application range: personal printers to large-scale data processing
Current speed range (approx.): daisy wheel /golf ball 5 cps to 35 cps line printers 200 - 2000 lines per minute	Current speed range (approx.): pin (**impact**) 25 cps to 250 cps ink jet (**or bubble jet**) 4 mins per page to 8+ ppm	Current speed range (approx.): laser 4 ppm to 40+ ppm (up to 2500+ lines per minute)
Resolution: daisy wheel /golf ball some proportional spacing	Resolution: ink jet (**or bubble jet**) 300 to 600 dots per inch	Resolution: laser 300 to 600 dots per inch

Table B5.1: Printers

Printer buffer

is a store, usually in the printer but can be in a separate box between the computer and printer, which receives the information for printing and stores it until it is printed. It is able to receive the information at a much higher speed than the printer can print, thereby freeing the computer from the printing task a little quicker.

Printer port

is the computer *port*, see page 154, at which a connection to a printer is made. In the computer, an *interface*, see page 154, provides the electronic link between the processor and the printer. When the computer prints, a *printer driver*, see page 137, changes the font and layout codes used in the computer into the form that the printer needs. Different kinds of printer may use the same port but each will probably require a different printer driver.

DIP switch

is a switch (often set out in groups of 4 or 8) on a printer that controls various aspects of the printer and how it should behave. They may control what language alphabet to use, what quality of print to print in, the size of print, etc. They may be located inside the printer, since once set they are not often altered. (DIP stands for Dual In-line Package.)

B6   Networks

Other terms and concepts related to networks and communications are to be found in A4 Communications, B7 Communications Devices and Control Devices.

Connecting pieces of communications and information equipment together in a network is not a new concept. The early telegraph systems, especially in America where the distances are so great, provided the stimulus for telegram services and the later development of telex communications, in which text information could be sent between any telex machines on the world-wide telex network using telephone lines. Passing messages internationally has been possible ever since the development of international cable links which began in the 19th century. For over 70 years the world's newspapers depended upon organisations that gathered news around the world and delivered it to their client newspapers through the telex network. These services are still provided by some of the same organisations but in addition there is now E-mail and other services linking computers around the world.

In a computer network a number of computers are connected together in order to exchange information. For example, an organisation having offices spread over a wide geographical area might install a network to enable employees to examine information held on computers in other offices many miles away.

The connections between computers may be wires, fibre optic cables, microwave links, communication via satellite or any combination of these. The interconnected collection of computers form the network. The computers may be large powerful machines, small personal computers or terminals. They will all be capable of running on their own but with the added advantage of being able to communicate with each other.

In a traditional network, users must explicitly log on (that is, identify themselves to the network) and explicitly move information around on the network by issuing the appropriate instructions. A **distributed system** is normally thought of as a network in which the existence of the other machines is not obvious to the user. Programs and data held on other machines can be used as though they were held locally on the user's computer.

A distinction is usually made between networks of computers that are all situated relatively close to each other - for example in the same building or cluster of buildings - known as a **Local Area Network** (a LAN) and those in which the computers are geographically remote, known as a **Wide Area Network** (a WAN).

A network offers the possibility of sharing work between the different resources available. For example, if one computer has a heavy load of processing, some of the work can be moved to another machine on the network. A network makes all the resources of the network (programs, data and equipment, such as printers and disk drives) available to the whole network without regard to the physical location of either the resource or the user.

Reliability is another advantage of networking. The effect of hardware failures can be reduced by switching work from a failed device to one that is still functioning. This can be particularly valuable in systems such as banking where it is important that the system can continue operating even if there are some hardware failures.

Networks of small computers can be a cheaper way of providing computer power than a single large machine. If a network of small machines has access to outside facilities, whose use may need to be purchased, the potential of the network is greatly enhanced. Linking a network to other networks, which are themselves linked to yet further networks, makes it theoretically possible to have the whole of world knowledge available to any computer on such a network.

The INTERNET is an implementation of this concept. It works because there are thousands of networks each connected to other networks in such a way that it is possible for messages (data) to be sent from a computer on one of the networks to any computer on any other network, provided that both networks have access to the Internet. How such data travels through this 'network of networks' is illustrated in Figure A4.2: *The life story of an E-mail message*, page 21.

Network
including: distributed network
is a linked set of computer systems capable of sharing computer power and resources such as printers, large disk drives, CD-ROM and other databases. Sometimes network is used to mean the arrangement of links between the equipment that form the network. See *network topology*, below.

In a ***distributed network*** the sharing of resources is arranged by the (network) operating system without any action being required by the user.

Local Area Network (LAN)

is a network in which the computer systems are all situated relatively close to each other, for example in the same building or cluster of buildings, such as a school. Since the distances involved are small, direct physical connection is possible. The network connections are normally wire cables, such as coaxial cable, but fibre optic cable is being increasingly used.

Wide Area Network (WAN)

is a network in which the computers are geographically remote. Wide area networks make use of a range of connection methods including communication satellites.

Network topology

including: bus network, ring (sometimes called loop) network, star network, hub, nexus, FDDI (fibre distributed data interface) backbone
is the theoretical arrangement of components of a network. The actual arrangement will almost certainly be determined by the buildings or other locations for the parts of the network. The network descriptions indicate how the devices on the network, the computers, printers, servers, etc., are connected to each other. Since networks communicate serially, the actual connections will be capable of *serial data transmission*, see page 154.

A ***bus network*** has each of the devices connected directly to a main communications line, called a bus, along which signals are sent. The bus will frequently be a twin cable of some kind, for example coaxial cable.

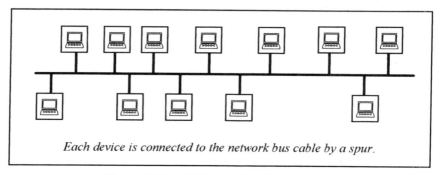

Each device is connected to the network bus cable by a spur.

Figure B6.1: A bus network with spurs

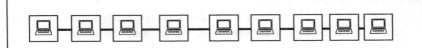

Each device has the network cable going into its network interface and out to the network interface of the next device.

Figure B6.2: A bus network

A **ring network** (sometimes called a **loop network**) has each of the devices on the network connected to a ring (or loop) communications line around which signals are sent. The devices may be connected to the ring by spurs, as in Figure B6.3, or the connections may pass through the network interface in each device, as in Figure B6.4; in this case, provision has to be made for the system to continue to work if one of the devices is switched off or fails to function properly.

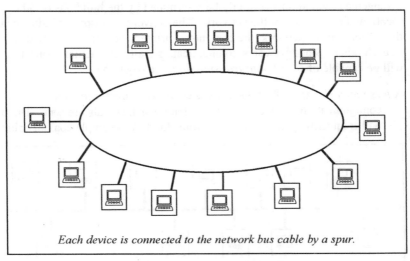

Each device is connected to the network bus cable by a spur.

Figure B6.3: A ring network with spurs

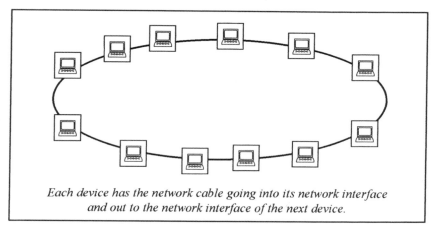

*Each device has the network cable going into its network interface
and out to the network interface of the next device.*

Figure B6.4: *A ring network*

A *star network* has all the network devices connected to one central computer
which is often used as the *file server* machine (see below). The centre of
the network, often called the *hub* or *nexus*, is a computer which has
separate connections to each computer or terminal.

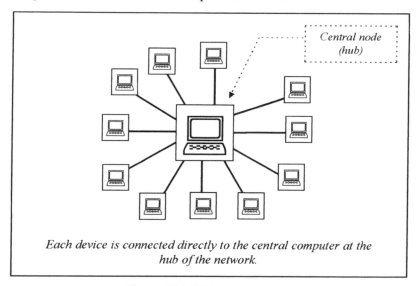

*Each device is connected directly to the central computer at the
hub of the network.*

Figure B6.5: *A star network*

A *FDDI backbone* is a high-speed communication link used to provide the
basis for a network consisting of small sub-networks. The connections are

fibre optic cable. *FDDI (fibre distributed data interface)* is an ANSI defined standard for high-speed fibre optic cable communications with transmission speeds of 100 Mbps.

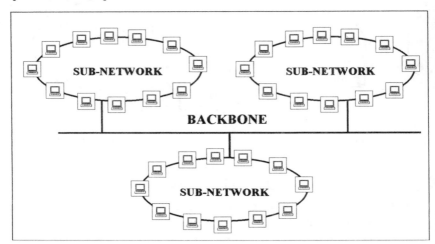

Figure B6.6: A backbone with three sub-networks

Cluster
including: cluster controller
is a group of computers in the same physical area, possibly on a network. A *cluster controller* is the computer acting as controller for the cluster. See also *network controller*, page 104.

Token ring network
including: token, Cambridge ring
is a *ring network* (see above) in which information is sent around the ring as variable-sized packets of data. In addition to the data, a packet will contain the address of the sender and the destination address. The *token*, which is a signal that passes round the network, can be thought of as a carrier for the packet. For a packet to travel round the ring it has to be attached to a token. This is a method of avoiding data packets colliding on the ring and creating unreadable signals. In principle, the packet travels round the ring attached to the token until it is taken off at the destination address or it returns unread to the sender, where it is taken off as unread. The token then becomes free and continues round the ring ready to have another package to be attached to it by one of the network devices. The token continually circulates around the ring

picking up, carrying and dropping packets off at their destinations. Generally there is only one token.

A *Cambridge ring* is a token ring network which has a number of tokens travelling around the network passing each device at equal time internals. A network device wishing to send a packet simply attaches it to the first available free token. The data transmission capacity of a Cambridge ring is much greater than a simple token ring network.

The network topology for token ring networks is shown in Figure B6.4, page 147.

Network number

including: station number

is the unique number assigned to a network when it is set up. All computers on the network have their own *station number* within the network, which is assigned through software. In addition, the network interface fitted in the computer has a unique number permanently stored in it. Communication between networks requires these unique numbers to ensure that messages get to the correct station in the correct network, since it is now possible for any network to communicate with any other network.

Econet

is an obsolete local area networking system designed to provide cheap computer networking for BBC and some Acorn microcomputers. Both the hardware (the cabling and computer interfaces) and the software (the *network operating system*, page 152) were non-standard and only worked with those computers. It has been used in a large number of British schools.

Ethernet

is a popular general-purpose *local area network* (see above). The network can be used by different types of computer system, even at the same time. Network interfaces are available from many manufacturers. It uses either wire connections (coaxial or twisted pair cable) or fibre optic cable. The software which makes up the *network operating system* (see below) has to be bought separately. Ethernet networks are frequently used in offices and schools. The transmission rate is 10 Mbits/sec and it uses the principles of carrier sense multiple access/collision detection which reduces the risk of one set of transmitted signals interfering with other transmissions.

Peer-to-peer network
including: client station
is a description of a very simple network which provides shared resources, such as printers and storage, but may offer little in the way of additional facilities, such as file security. The name comes from the fact that all the computers on these networks have similar specifications and that all stations on the network have equal status. For example one station may act as a file server, another as the printer server, but both of them are also network stations capable of being used as client stations. A computer on the network, which is available for use by users of the network, is called a *client station*. See also *terminal* and *server*, below.

Client-server relationship
is a method of network organisation in which stations make use of resources available at one or more *servers* (see below). This is the kind of organisation seen in a *star network* (see above), in which one computer has the role of central resource manager for the network. But other forms of network can also operate with a client-server relationship.

Distributed processing
is the sharing of data processing tasks between physically separated processors on a network. The sharing of tasks is managed by the network operating system software. See also *network operating system* and *server*, below.

Terminal
also called: network terminal, network station, station
including: point-of-sale (POS) terminal
is a computer or computer-controlled device operating on a network. A stand-alone computer used to provide resources for the whole network is a form of terminal which is often called a *(network) station*. See also *server*, below.

A network may have a variety of different kinds of equipment connected to it. For example, a supermarket network will probably have standard computers for its offices as well as the *point-of-sale (POS) terminals* (the checkouts) all connected on the same network. This may be linked to a wider network for the whole supermarket chain. A point-of-sale terminal will have a variety of functions, which may include *electronic funds transfer* (see page 20), as well as *bar code scanning* (see page 106) combined with getting the costs from a database on the network to produce the customer's bill.

Server

including: file server, printer server, printer spooler, CD-ROM server,
database server
is a station on a *network* (see above) which provides a resource that can be
used by any authorised *station* (see *terminal*, above). There are a number of
types of server.

A *file server* provides central disk storage for any users of the network. The
file server software identifies each user's files separately so that other
users cannot use them. Users can access their own files from any client
station on the network.

A *printer server* allows all the client stations to use a printer controlled by it
and usually provides the facilities of a *printer spooler* which is software
which stores data ready for printing. When the complete data to be
printed has been received from a program, the printer spooler can send
this data to the printer. Several programs or terminals can send data at
the same time for printing.

A *CD-ROM server* allows all the client stations to obtain data from a
CD-ROM disk currently being used by the CD-ROM server computer.
Often a CD-ROM server will have access to many CD-ROM disks, either
from a collection of several CD-ROM players, or from a *CD-ROM*
jukebox (see page 113).

A *database server* manages a large database. Client stations can access data
in the database and, if authorised, can maintain the database. The
database processing is usually carried out by the server, with the query
being sent by a client station to the server and the results assembled by
the server and returned to the client station. This form of *client-server*
relationship (see above) can ensure the consistency of the database, even
in the distributed environment of a *peer-to-peer network* (see above).

Any expensive resource can be made available to a large number of users by a
server computer. Other examples are a teletext server, which makes available
the current data being broadcast by teletext services; a viewdata server, which
provides and manages a local viewdata service for the network; a mail server
to manage the electronic mail for the network; or even a weather station server
obtaining and distributing current local instrument readings or satellite weather
data.

Work station

is **either** a *station* on a network (see *terminal*, above), **or** a location where a
computer, with its associated equipment, is used, such as a designer's work
area; this kind of work station may be on a network or not.

Network operating system

including: Appletalk, NFS, Novell Netware, Windows for Workgroups, Unix
is the software needed to enable a computer to communicate with other
computers (stations) using a network. All computers on a network must have
the same network operating system software to be able to communicate
through the network. Additional software is required for any servers. In
particular, a file server needs additional software to enable it to provide secure
data storage for users. Widely used network operating systems include
Appletalk, NFS (Acorn computers), *Novell Netware, Windows for
Workgroups* and *Unix*.

Network accounting software

provides statistics about the use of a network by its users. This may be about
the use made of terminals on a multi-user computer system or about the use of
facilities on a *peer-to-peer network* (see above). The information can be used
to charge users for their use of resources or to monitor improper use of the
network.

  The information recorded can include such things as the connection time and
the processor time used, a list of times and dates when the computer has been
used on a multi-user system, disk storage space used, printer use, and E-mail
use on a peer-to-peer network.

  The accounting software can present the overall activity on the network in a
variety of ways (tables, graphs or a log) and thus assist the network manager
to optimise the system and, possibly, devise charging structures.

Value Added Network Service (VANS)

is a wide area network with additional facilities such as a centrally provided
database or information system for which users pay charges, which are usually
based on their use of the facilities.

Gateway

is a link between two dissimilar computer systems, which may be local area
networks. The communications between the systems are usually sent via
public telecommunications links. The gateway converts the data passing
through it into the formats required for each system; in addition, it can monitor
usage and limit access between the systems to authorised users. See also
bridge, page 159.

B7   Communications Devices and Control Devices

*This section is concerned with terms used in describing the
transmission of data between computers within networks and
terms found in the study of control systems. Other related
terms may be found in A4 Communications, A9 Control,
B2 Peripherals, B6 Networks.*

Communications and control require that information is passed rapidly and
accurately between parts of a system. The origins of present-day
communication systems are the electric telegraph in which signals were sent as
electric pulses, the telephone in which sound is passed as a varying electric
current, and radio in which the signals are sent as electromagnetic radiation.

Modern communications systems are highly reliable, accurate and
affordable. From the earliest days of computers until the late 1980s it was
necessary to install special quality telephone lines between linked computers.
Now it is possible to use standard voice quality lines for connecting computers
and remote devices. This is partly due to the use of digital signal systems and
partly due to the use of more reliable materials and devices for the
transmission of signals in the public communications systems. The installation
of digital telephone exchanges in many parts of the world, and the use of radio
links where cables are not available, mean that it is impossible for a user to
know whether a link between two telephones or two computers is by cables or
via some terrestrial or satellite radio link. Where public communication links
are not available, private links are installed.

The materials for connecting computers are wires of some form, fibre optic
cables, radio links or infra-red radiation. Each has its advantages and its
disadvantages. If wires or optic cables are used, then the individual locations
of equipment may be restricted to sites served by the cables; if infra-red links
are used then receivers and transmitters have to be in sight of each other; if
radio is used then privacy may not be easily achieved. At present, nearly all
local area networks are linked by some form of wire cable. Where these
connect into the wider world, they require some device to make the connections
to the outside world. These connecting devices arrange for the signals to be
sent in an appropriate form, at the correct speed and with the necessary
destination information attached. The computer user determines the content
and destination of the messages but the linking devices determine the way in
which the messages are sent and often the route.

Interface

including: serial interface, parallel interface, Centronics interface
is the hardware and any associated software needed for communication
between processors and peripheral devices or between parts of a network. Any
peripheral connected to a computer must be connected through an interface.
There are a number of internationally defined interface standards.
Each type of computer may require slightly different interface designs because
of the computer's internal design, but the roles they perform are the same.

Serial interfaces are used for *serial data transmission* (see below).

Parallel interfaces are used for *parallel data transmission* (see below). One
parallel interface, the *Centronics interface*, is often used for printers.

Interface board

also known as: interface card
is the hardware for an *interface* (see above) mounted on a small printed circuit
board, which can easily be plugged into connection points inside a computer.

Port

including: serial port, parallel port
is a connection point or socket which allows the internal circuits of a computer
to be connected to some external device or system. If the interface is serial
then the port is referred to as the *serial port*; if the interface is parallel then the
port is called the *parallel port*. See also *printer port*, page 142.

Data transmission

including: synchronous, asynchronous, parallel, serial transmission
is the passing of data from one device to another. This may be between parts
of a computer system or between computers in a network.

Data transmission may have a number of properties, which include:
- the transmission may be synchronised or unsynchronised
- it may be parallel or serial.

In *synchronous transmission* all the data transfers are timed to coincide with
  a clock pulse but in *asynchronous transmission* each character is sent as
  soon as it becomes available without waiting for a synchronisation signal.
In *parallel data transmission* the bits for a character are sent simultaneously
  along separated data lines. This needs one line per bit plus one extra line.
In *serial data transmission* the bits for a character are sent one after another
  along the same data line. This requires only two lines.

In practice most systems use more than the required minimum number of lines.

Communications channel
also known as: data channel, data carrier, data link
including: data transmission
is a communication circuit along which data, in coded form, may be transmitted between two points; it may consist of more than one line. **Data transmission** is the process of using a data link. See also *facsimile transmission*, page 22.

Modem (MOdulator-DEModulator)
is a data communications device for sending and receiving data between computers over telephone circuits. It converts the digital signals from the computer into audio tones for transmission over ordinary voice quality telephone lines and converts incoming audio signals into digital signals for the computer. It is normally plugged directly into a standard telephone socket.

Fax modem
is a modem with the ability to send documents as if it were a fax machine.

Fax (facsimile) machine
is a machine for transmitting and receiving copies of paper document pages over telephone circuits. The process involves scanning a document and transmitting the resulting data to another fax machine which prints the copy.

Terminal adapter
including: ISDN (Integrated Services Digital Network)
is an interface which is plugged into a microcomputer serial port to link into the ISDN (Integrated Services Digital Network).

ISDN is an internationally agreed set of standards for world-wide communications for speech, and other data, with the simplicity of access that current telephone dialling systems provide.

Private Branch Exchange (PBX)
including: Private Automatic Branch Exchange (PABX)
is a private telephone exchange. It provides the interface between a group of telephone extensions and the public network lines. There is usually a facility which allows any extension to dial any other extension directly and to dial into the public network using only a simple connect code and the outside number. Normally, external callers only get the operator unless they know the direct dial number for an individual extension.

Digital *PABXs* can control and interconnect a mix of telephones, fax machines, teletext devices and computers all operating at different bit rates.

Multiplexor

sometimes spelt: multiplexer
including: time division multiplexor (TDM), time slice, statistical
multiplexor, intelligent time division multiplexor, frequency division
multiplexor (FDM)
is a device that receives data from several independent sources for
transmission along a single route to a single destination. A two-way
communication multiplexor must be able to separate signals for each of the
destinations. The multiplexor for the host computer in Figure B7.1 could be a
front-end processor (see page 103).

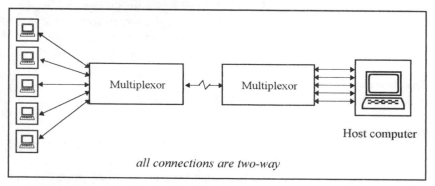

Figure B7.1: *Multiplexors connecting remote workstations to a computer*

A *time division multiplexor* (*TDM*) transmits the signals from two or more
  sources in successive short time intervals, called *time slices*. Each source
  gets the same duration of time interval. Where the multiplexor time
  allocation is proportional to the activity of each source, it is called a
  statistical multiplexor, or an *intelligent time division multiplexor.*
A *frequency division multiplexor* (*FDM*) uses the available route link to
  transmit the data from the different sources at the same time. This is
  achieved by dividing the available channel bandwidth into a number of
  narrow bands, each of which is used for a separate transmission but at a
  slower speed.

Signal concentrator

also known as: message concentrator, concentrator
is any device, such as a multiplexor, which is used to enable a single channel
to be used for carrying multiple communications.

Wire connector

including: copper cable, coaxial cable, twisted pair (TP), unshielded twisted pair (UTP)

is a standard form of wire cable used to provide the connections in a network. *Copper cables* are commonly used as connectors for local area networks, since they are readily available and have suitable electrical characteristics. Various types of copper cable are used, including:

Coaxial cable, which is made to a variety of specifications, is the same kind of cable that is used for connecting a television aerial to a television set. It has two conductors. One is a wire down the centre of the cable, which may be a single strand, insulated from the second, which is made up of many strands braided around the insulation for the inner wire.

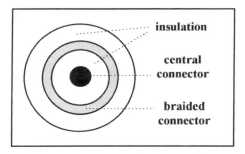

Figure B7.2: *Section of coaxial cable*

Twisted pair (*TP*) cable is commonly used for data transmission. In its simplest form it is a pair of insulated copper wires twisted together surrounded by a copper braid and external insulation. Some cables are made up of a number of twisted pairs surrounded by an overall (earthed) braid screen. In another form, stranded copper wires are twisted together in pairs with an earth wire. These pairs may be grouped to form a single multi-connector cable. These cables all have different specifications and, used in the correct situation, provide minimum interference data transmission.

Unshielded twisted pair (*UTP*) is similar to the twisted pair cables described above, but have no earthed shield. In suitable circumstances they can be used for data transmission.

Fibre optic cable

also known as: optical fibre

is a very fine glass strand that allows rapid transmission of data, using modulated light beams. It is usual to put many strands together in a single cable, each one capable of carrying one or more data signals. Fibre optic cable provides interference-free, secure data transmission and, unlike metal wires, is not subject to corrosion.

Wireless communication
including: infra-red, microwave transmission, satellite
covers a whole range of possible methods of data transmission, which can be used for linking computers within networks or for links within computer systems.

Infra-red communication uses the same systems as domestic remote control of televisions. Examples of its use include the control of robotic devices and remote keyboards. It is necessary for there to be direct unobstructed line of sight between the transmitter and the receiver. Strong sunlight will interfere with infra-red signals.

Microwave transmission is used as a method of communication within public telephone services. Many organisations use private installations to transmit data between key sites. Unlike the cellular phone systems which are broadcast systems, microwave transmissions use highly directional transmitters and receivers with dish aerials.

Satellite links are used for international communications by many providers of public telephone services. Unlike satellite broadcast systems, these links use highly directional, narrow beam, two-way transmissions. A single channel is capable of simultaneously carrying a very large number of separate transmissions.

Cable TV
sometimes: cable
is a form of communications network that provides television programmes into consumer's homes through underground cables. The cables are usually coaxial cable, but some installations use fibre optic cable. The cables installed for cable TV could easily be used for a variety of other communications purposes and could become part of an *ISDN* (see above) system.

Terminator
is a device fitted to the end of a network cable which is not plugged into a network terminal. In some network systems, any cable end not terminated can cause the network communications to fail. Similarly SCSI (Small Computer Systems Interface) cables need to be properly terminated. A terminator may look rather like a cable connector with only one socket, its purpose being to prevent signal reflections in the, otherwise unterminated, cable.

Repeater

including: multi-part repeater, router, bridge, brouter
is a device to link two cable segments. Because of the loss of signal strength in network cables, a repeater amplifies the signals it receives before passing them on.

A *multi-part repeater* can be used to create a spur off the network.

A *router* is a form of repeater. In some systems it is merely used as another name for a repeater; in others, it is a device that identifies the destinations of messages and sends them on via an appropriate route.

A *bridge* is a connection between two local area networks. The use of a bridge produces a logical network, which appears to all users as a single network although it may be made up of several physically distinct networks. All users have access to all the resources on the resulting enlarged network, in particular the various *servers* (see page 151). See also *gateway*, page 152.

A *brouter* is a device which combines the functions and properties of a bridge and a repeater on a local area network.

Handshake

is the exchange of signals between devices to establish their readiness to send or receive data, for example the transmission of data from a computer to a printer. Handshaking is one of a number of methods of ensuring that both the sender and receiver are ready before transmission begins.

Signal converter

including: analog signal, digital signal, Analog to Digital (A-to-D or A/D) converter, digitising, Digital to Analog (D-to-A or D/A) converter
is a device which converts serial signals from one form to another. Signals may be *digital*, consisting of discrete bit patterns, or *analog*, consisting of a continuously variable voltage. Both analog and digital signals are used to represent data. Some devices generate analog signals or need to be supplied with data in analog form, while others generate or have to be supplied with data in digital form.

An *Analog-to-Digital (A-to-D) converter* converts analog signals into digital signals for subsequent processing. This conversion is sometimes called *digitising*. For example, the analog output from a microphone has to be digitised before it can be stored or processed by a computer.

A *Digital-to-Analog (D-to-A) converter* converts serial digital signals into analog signals. For example, the digital data for a computer display has to be converted into analog signals if it is to be used as input to a television.

Signal level

including: signal amplifier, signal booster

is the measure of the strength of a communications signal. In the same way that sound and light become weaker with distance, electrical signals passing down a wire become weaker as they travel along the wire. For this reason *signal amplifiers* or *boosters* are built into communications networks at appropriate intervals. These increase the signal level before passing the signal on to the next part of the network.

Baud

including: baud rate, bits per second (bps), bit rate, bytes per second (bps), characters per second (cps)

is the unit used to measure the speed (the *baud rate*) of serial data transmission, for example the transmission of data along a telephone line or the speed of serial transmission to a printer. Generally, one baud is one bit per second, but it is important to note that there is no simple relationship between baud rate and the rate of data transfer between devices. Under any communications protocol additional bits have to be transmitted to provide start and stop bits, error detection and other communications controls. In addition, methods of communication, such as multiphase signalling, and data compression can both increase the amount of data that is transmitted in a given time.

   Other measures of speed of data transfer are:

Bits per second (bps), sometimes called the *bit rate,* is a measure of the speed with which data moves between various parts of a computer. High bit rates are given in Kbits/s (2^{10} = 1024 bps) or Mbits/s (2^{20} = 1048576 bps). [Note: sometimes *bps* is taken to mean *bytes per second* which is normally the same as characters per second.]

Characters per second (cps) is a measure of the speed of character data transfer between devices. It is frequently also given as a measure of the speed of printers.

Transducer

is an electronic component which converts one form of energy to another. The term is generally applied to devices which produce electricity rather than those which convert electricity into another form of energy. For example, a thermistor converts temperature into a voltage, a photo cell converts brightness of illumination into a voltage.

Sampler
also known as: digital sampler
is an electronic circuit which takes samples of an electronic signal at intervals and stores them for future processing. In particular, they are used to take frequent measurements of analog signals for converting an analog signal into a digital signal, when it is known as a digital sampler.

Sensor
including: analog sensor, digital sensor, passive device, active device
is a *transducer* (see above) which responds to some physical property such as pressure, rate of flow, humidity, the proximity of ferrous metal. The sensor produces an electrical output which is either *analog* or *digital*. Some sensors, called *passive devices*, require no external electrical source. Those which require an external voltage are called *active devices*.

Servo mechanism
also known as: servo
is a mechanical mechanism for remote control of machines. A simple form is the motors which operate the control surfaces of a radio-controlled model aircraft, where the person flying the model plays an active part continuously adjusting the position of the control levers. Servos can be controlled electronically through computer circuits which may incorporate feedback to achieve automatic control; in these situations human participation may be very limited.

Actuator
is any device which can be operated by signals from a computer or control system causing physical movement. For example, devices for opening windows in a computer-controlled ventilation system.

Stepper motor
sometimes: stepping motor
is an electric motor which moves in small rotational steps. Suitably controlled and geared, a stepper motor can provide very small discrete movements, for example the movement of the paper rollers and the print head in a printer. The control circuits may well involve the use of *feedback* (see page 39).

B8   Systems Design and Development

*Other related material will be found in Section A16 User
Documentation, Section B9 Systems Documentation and B10
Systems Software and Programming Languages. Those seeking
to find a wider selection of terms associated with the
development of systems and for terms used in computer
programming should consult the full edition of the BCS
Glossary (ISBN 0-582-27544-X).*

The design of computer information systems, which may include specifying
hardware, software and other systems, is a task that requires considerable
management and discipline. The construction of large, complex computer systems
(on which safety as well as profits may depend) is very similar to the construction
of civil engineering projects such as bridges or buildings. What used to be known
as 'programming' is part of an activity which is often referred to as 'software
engineering'.

The development of a computer system to meet the requirements of a large
organisation needs a specification for the complete system (hardware and other
software, communications systems and even the training needs of the staff who
will use the system). In contrast, the development of a general-purpose package
such as a desk-top publishing system will begin by defining the types of computer
and operating system on which the package is intended to work.

Each of these tasks will be carried out by a team including software engineers.
These teams will often be very large and the members of the team may change
before the task is completed. The tasks for the team have to be clearly defined and
schedules decided if the work is to be completed satisfactorily and on time.

Throughout the development careful records have to be kept of what the
software does and how it should be used. Tests have to be established for the
software as it is developed and at completion. When the project is completed,
documentation has to be put together which will allow users to understand how the
system is to be used. In addition there has to be technical documentation written
with the needs of other software and hardware engineers in mind, such as
developers of hardware on which the software will be used.

Applications system design

including: systems design, systems analysis, feasibility study, system specification, functional specification

is the process involved in the design of applications software packages. This process is often referred to as *systems design*. Typically the process begins with an analysis of any existing system and of the requirements of the new system (*systems analysis*). A *feasibility study* of potential computer involvement may be made, estimating costs, effort, effectiveness, reliability and the benefits to be expected from a new system. The desired system will be specified in a *systems specification* that sets out the hardware and software requirements, and the organisational and human implications. This may include a separate *functional specification* that describes exactly how the system will behave. Only when all these stages have been completed will work begin on the production of the software.

System development cycle

is the complete cycle of activities involved in creating a new or modified computer system. See also *applications system design*, above and *implementation*, below.

SYSTEM DEVELOPMENT CYCLE

Stage	Description
Specification	identifying the user's requirements
Analysis and design	examining the user's requirements and creating a design to satisfy them
Implementation (of the design)	producing the software (and any necessary hardware) to the design created in the previous stage
Testing	ensuring that the implemented design works
Implementation (of the system)	making the system work for the user, perhaps within an existing system
Documentation	creating the user and technical documentation for the whole system

Each stage involves iterative review until the result is acceptable.

Figure B8.1: System development cycle

Software

including: applications program, applications package, generic software, productivity tool

consists of programs, routines and procedures (together with their associated documentation) which can be run on a computer system.

An ***applications program*** is a computer information system designed to carry out a task (such as keeping accounts, editing text) which would need to be carried out even if computers did not exist.

An ***applications package*** is a complete set of applications programs together with the associated documentation (see *user documentation*, page 88). Where the application is appropriate to many areas, it is usual to describe it as ***generic software*** or as a ***productivity tool***. For example, *word processing* (see page 8) can be used in personal correspondence, the production of business 'form letters', academic research, compilation of glossaries, writing books etc.

Operational mode

including: batch processing, transaction processing, multi-access, time-sharing, real-time system, interactive processing, remote access, tele-processing, off-line processing, on-line processing, time-sharing

is the way a computer system is used and operated. Decisions about operational modes are made during system design. Often the *operating system* (see page 176) manages the functioning of the operational modes in use.

The different types of processing are not necessarily exclusive, and more than one might be applicable to any particular computer system.

In ***batch processing*** all the data to be input is collected together before being processed as a single efficient operation. This method is also used when computer users submit individual jobs which are processed together as a batch.

Transaction processing deals with each set of data from a user as it is submitted. This is normally used in commercial systems where a transaction may be a booking, an order or an invoice. Each transaction is completed before the next is begun.

Multi-access systems allow several users apparently to have individual control of the computer at the same time. One method of implementing a multi-access system is by allocating a period of time to each user, this is called ***time-sharing***.

Real-time system is one which can react fast enough to influence behaviour in the outside world; for example, this is necessary in air-traffic control systems and desirable in on-line ticket reservation systems.

Interactive processing provides the user with direct, immediate responses from the system. There is often some kind of dialogue with the system. Examples include the booking of airline tickets, requesting information about a bank account through a cash dispensing machine.

Remote access or *tele-processing* is the use of a geographically remote computer system via communications links.

Off-line processing occurs when devices are not under the immediate control of the main computer, for example data entry to disk or tape storage.

On-line processing allows the user to interact directly with the main computer.

Implementation

including: parallel running, pilot running, direct changeover, big-bang, phased implementation

is the process of starting to use an information system in a real situation after having designed and developed it. It may enable final testing in a real situation. Four different approaches are used depending on the size of the system and the properties of the data being processed.

Parallel running requires the new system to operate for a short period of time alongside the older system. The results can be compared to ensure that the new system is working correctly.

Pilot running requires the new system to operate alongside the old system but only processing part of the data. The results can be compared to check that the system works correctly but pilot running cannot test how the system will operate with the larger quantities of data of the real situation.

Direct changeover or *big-bang* requires that the new system replaces the old system without any overlap. In some cases the nature of the system prevents parallel or pilot running and a direct changeover is the only option, for example an emergency control system.

Phased implementation involves replacing some parts of the old system while other parts continue to use the old system. This enables training and installation to be spread over a longer period of time. An example is a supermarket chain, which would not install a new system in all its branches at the same time, but phase it in as the branches are refurbished. The first phase of the implementation could also be used as parallel running.

Modular design
including: module
is a method of organising the design of a large system into self-contained parts, *modules*, which can be developed simultaneously. Modules have clearly defined relationships with the other parts of the system, which enables them to be independently designed, written and maintained.

Audit trail
including: journal file
is an automatic record made (in a *journal file*) of any transactions carried out by a computer system, such as updates to files. This may be required for legal reasons (so that the auditors can confirm the accuracy of the company accounts); for security reasons (so that data maliciously or accidentally deleted can be recovered); or simply to monitor the performance of the system.

Benchmark
including: acceptance testing
is a standard computer task, designed to allow measurements to be made of computer performance. Benchmark tasks can be used to compare the performance of different software or hardware. Examples of tasks are: how long it takes to re-format a 40-page word processed document, how many pages can be printed in one minute, how long it takes to save 1000 database records to disk. Users seeking to buy software or hardware may be able to obtain some information about the performance of possible purchases.

Benchmarks may also figure in *acceptance testing* of a computer system, by specifying performance that must be achieved before the system is considered finished.

Default
including: default option, default value
is an assumption made by computer software in the absence of explicit instruction to the contrary. This may be a *default option* – your files are listed in alphabetical order, unless you request date or size order – or a *default value* – the computer prints one copy of a document, unless you request multiple copies. The best software is designed so that the most frequently-used options are all available as defaults, so that users are not troubled by the continued need to specify such values. It is often possible for users to customise software, by selecting their own choice of defaults.

Configuration management

is the automatic tracking and monitoring of changes to software during development, so that everyone involved is aware of the features of the latest version.

Software characteristics

including: ease of maintenance, ease of use, flexibility, portability, port, (hardware) platform, reliability, robustness
are the general properties (which may be good or bad) of programs or systems, which determine how successful the program may be in general use. The good properties that programmers will attempt to produce are:

Ease of maintenance allows modifications that have to be made during the life of a system to be carried out easily and cheaply. Program maintenance is a major expense in the use of a computer system. *Modular design* (see above) enables software to be produced in a way that makes it easy to maintain.

Ease of use means that users will be able to operate the program with limited training and support.

Flexibility is the ability of a program or system to be easily reconfigured by the user or adapted for use in a different situation. This may enable a program or system to be sold more widely or to be adapted to changing circumstances.

Portability is the ability of a program or system to be used on different computer hardware. Many large commercial systems remain in use for much longer than the original hardware and will be adapted or *ported* to new types of computer hardware, thus saving the expense of rewriting the system. Most software packages will only work on particular combinations of hardware and operating system, which are sometimes referred to as *(hardware) platforms*.

Reliability is how well a program or system operates without stopping due to design faults.

Robustness is the ability of a program or system to cope with errors and mishaps during program execution without producing wrong results or stopping. Events (such as a jammed printer) should not make the computer system fail. If failures do occur, errors can be introduced which can lead to customer dissatisfaction.

Developmental testing
including: alpha test, beta test

Commercial software is traditionally developed to an incomplete state, with some questions of design, command sequences, defaults, etc. left unresolved. It is then issued in an ***alpha test*** version to a restricted audience of testers within the developer's own company. When the results of this in-house testing have been studied and appropriate changes made, a ***beta test*** version is released to a number of privileged customers in exchange for their constructive comments. Beta test versions are usually close to the finally released product. They are made available to computer magazine reviewers, authors of instructional manuals and developers of associated software or hardware products.

Test plan
including: test data

is the schedule for testing a program or a system. It is usually a table showing each item which needs to be tested. The test plan should cover every possible type of input including those which may be made by mistake, such as values that are too large, too small or just silly. The data used, when following a test plan, is called ***test data***. Both the test plan and the test data need to be available as part of the documentation of the program or system. For a program, the test data will show the inputs to the program and specify what the results should be if the program works correctly.

Run
including: run-time, run-time error

is putting a program or information system into action so that it can perform the data processing it was designed to do.

Run-time is the time during which a program or information system is in operation. Often data has to be provided during run-time and the full behaviour of the program can only be observed when the system is operating.

Run-time errors are errors detected during run-time. These errors may occur either when software is being developed or when completed systems are being used. Run-time errors are often due to external effects not allowed for by the program, such as lack of memory or unusual data.

B9   *Systems Documentation*

*This section is concerned with the written comments and
graphical illustrations which form the description of a system.
Related topics can be found in A16 User Documentation,
B8 Systems Design and Development.*

Software systems will require some modification during their lifetime. If this is to
be done satisfactorily, it is vital that good, complete and understandable
documentation is available. Requests to modify software may arise for a number
of reasons and the original team that did the analysis and design, and the
implementation, may not be available to carry out modifications to the system.
This makes it all the more important that good, up-to-date documentation is
available throughout the life of the system.

A standard form of documentation may be followed, which will specify, at
various levels of detail, what documentation should be produced and how it should
be presented.

Documentation produced at the design and analysis stage will include the
agreed requirements specification for the system. As the design develops, a range
of diagrams will be produced. These will show such things as the relationships
between the data and the processes that manipulate the data.

The design task is tackled by gradually breaking it down into smaller parts
(sub-tasks). At each stage diagrams are used to indicate how tasks are done and
how the different tasks are related. Often diagrams use different shapes to indicate
the use of a particular device or medium, in the same kind of way that icons are
often used in a graphical user interface. As programs are designed and developed
there will be other documentation to describe each program. All of this will form
part of the maintenance documentation.

The full description of a system will include the *user documentation* (see page
86) and probably training material for users of the system.

Flowchart
including: flow line
is a graphical representation of the operations involved in a process or system.
Flowchart symbols (see below) are used to represent particular operations or data,
and *flow lines*, which connect the flowchart symbols, indicate the sequence of
operations or the flow of data. Flow lines may use arrows to indicate sequence, or
a top-down, left-right convention may apply if there are no arrows.

Flowchart symbol

is a symbol used in a flowchart diagram. Different shapes indicate the various kinds of activity described by the diagram. Sometimes highly formalised shapes are used, each having a specific meaning; in other situations very simple boxes with words are used. Provided the meaning is clear, either method is an equally acceptable way of representing a process or system.

An example of how these symbols might be used is given in Figure B9.1, below, which uses formal shapes.

System flowchart

also called: data flow diagram (DFD), data flowchart, system flowchart diagram, system diagram

is a *flowchart* (see above) used to describe a complete data processing system. The flow of data through the operations is diagrammatically described, down to the level of the individual programs needed to achieve the system requirements. An example of a system flowchart is given in Figure B9.1, below, which uses formal shapes.

Program flowchart

is a *flowchart* (see above) used to describe a program and is usually constructed before programming starts. The sequence of operations is indicated by *flow lines* (see above) and actions are often indicated by *flowchart symbols* (see above).

Maintenance documentation

also known as: technical documentation
including: systems documentation, program documentation

is written for the computer professional rather than the system user. Some parts will be highly technical, for example, the specifications of peripherals and their configuration. The reader of this technical documentation will need to have expert knowledge. Technical documentation will include:

systems documentation which describes how the system was developed, what its parts are and how it should be used

program documentation which provides details of the individual programs which make up the software of the system.

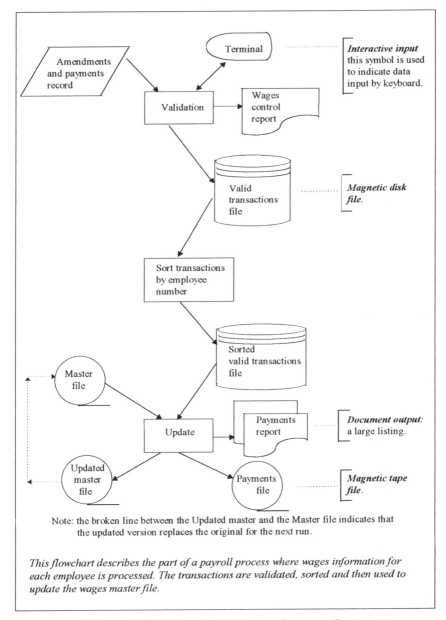

Note: the broken line between the Updated master and the Master file indicates that the updated version replaces the original for the next run.

This flowchart describes the part of a payroll process where wages information for each employee is processed. The transactions are validated, sorted and then used to update the wages master file.

Figure B9.1: *Flowchart of part of a payroll process*

B10   Systems Software and Programming Languages

Other related material will be found in Section B9 Systems Documentation.

A computer system requires software which enables users to operate the computer without having to know much about the processes that are going on all the time inside the computer. The software needed for this is called **systems software**. Essential systems software is purchased with the computer and other systems software may be purchased separately.

Part of this systems software will be **operating system software** which controls the vital parts of the computer's operation - using the keyboard, screen display, loading and saving files and printing are some examples.

Additional software, which is useful in the operation of the computer and makes using the computer easier, called **utility programs** or **library programs**, is also available.

It is usual for a computer system to be sold with some facility for writing programs. So there will normally be a **programming language** together with the appropriate **interpreter**, **compiler** or **assembler**.

Program

is a complete set of program statements, written in a *programming language* (see below), that can be executed by a computer to perform a task.

Systems program

is one of the programs that control the operation of a computer system. These enable the computer system to be developed and to work efficiently. Examples of systems programs are compilers, disk formatters, network software and print spoolers. Many systems programs are part of the *operating system* (see below).

Systems programs can be contrasted with *applications programs* (see page 164), which perform some task. These tasks, such as producing a letter, are not part of the actual operation of the computer.

Utility program

is a *systems program* (see above) designed to perform a commonplace task, for example the transfer of data from one storage device to another, sorting a set of data, or a disk editor for directly editing the contents of a disk.

Software library

also known as: library, program library

is a collection of software held either permanently accessible on backing store or on removable media such as tape or disk. It will include complete software packages as well as individual *utility programs* (see above).

Library program

is program available to all users of a multi-user computer system, typically to carry out common tasks (such as file maintenance) required by everyone. See also *software library*, above.

Programming language

including: computer language, high-level language, intermediate-level language, low-level language, machine code, machine language

is a language in which computer programs are written. Programming languages are often called *computer languages*.

Programming languages have been designed to satisfy many different needs. They can use different levels of complexity (often referred to as *high-*, *intermediate-* and *low-level languages*). The lower the language level, the closer to the way that computers actually work. The language in which the most detailed instructions are given to a computer is called a *machine code* or *machine language*

Programming languages exist for many different kinds of activity (for example, mathematical, graphical, writing teaching materials). All programs written in a programming language, other than machine code, will have to be translated (see *translator*, below) before they can be run on a computer. Information about some important programming languages is given in Table B10.1 (below).

Translator

including: assembler, compiler, interpreter

is a computer program used to convert a program from one (computer) language to another. There are three types of translators

Assemblers translate a program written in low-level languages called assembly languages into machine code.

Compilers translate a high-level language program into a computer's machine code or possibly some other low-level language.

Interpreters translate and execute a program one statement at a time. Interpreted languages may be either high-level or intermediate-level languages.

See also *programming language*, above.

Language	Date	derivation of name	translated	data
Ada	1975-83	after Countess Lovelace	compiled	numeric
ALGOL	1958-68	ALGOrithmic Language	compiled	numeric
APL	1957-68	A Programming Language	interpreted	numeric/ characters
BASIC	1964	Beginners All-purpose Symbolic Instruction Code	interpreted	numeric
C	1972	see notes	compiled	numeric/ text
COBOL	1959-60	COmmon Business Oriented Language	compiled	numeric/ strings
COMAL	1973	COMmon Algorithmic Language	interpreted	numeric
FORTH	late 1960's	pun on 'Fourth'	compiled	graphics
FORTRAN	1954-57	FORmula TRANslation	compiled	numeric
Lisp	1959	List Processing	interpreted	symbols
Logo	1966-68	Greek for 'thought'	interpreted	symbols/ graphics
Pascal	1968-71	after Blaise Pascal	compiled	numeric
PILOT	1968	Programmed Inquiry, Learning Or Teaching	interpreted	characters/ graphics
PL/1	1963-64	Programming Language 1	compiled	numeric/ strings
PROLOG	1972	PROgramming in LOGic	interpreted	symbols
RPG	1964	Report Program Generator	compiled	numeric/ strings
Simula	1965	from simulation	compiled	numeric/ symbolic
Smalltalk	1972-80	to emphasise nature of language interface	compiled	all types
SNOBOL	1962-68	StriNg Oriented SymBolic Language	compiled	symbolic

NOTES :

date is that of the initial development; most languages have been continuously improved since their invention.

translated indicates the most usual method, not necessarily the *only* one.

data is that type for which the language was originally intended– with the advent of the microcomputer, most languages have been enhanced to handle text and graphics.

Table B10.1: Programming languages

structure	ext	notes
imperative	no	mainly used for large military systems, sponsored by US Dept of Defense
imperative	no	originally for (paper) description of algorithms – an influential language with several distinct versions (Algol-60, Algol-68)
functional	yes	easier to write than to read; it uses symbols not always found on regular keyboards – requires large memory
imperative	no	easy to learn and (in modernised versions) the world's most frequently encountered programming language, especially on microcomputers
imperative	no	systems programming language, derived from 'B' which derived in turn from BCPL, which derived from CPL
imperative	no	easier to read than to write; large memory requirements, hence a mainframe language; highly structured data suited to business use
imperative	no	a Danish attempt to add structure to BASIC programming, which originally ignored data structuring
unique	yes	very different from other languages: used in control and graphics applications
imperative	no	mainstream scientific programming language; language still reflects punched-card input – too early to have been a structured language
functional	yes	artificial intelligence uses – an influential language, in that many other languages have been derived from it
functional	yes	based on Lisp, but noted for its 'turtle graphics' subset; popular in education, as it 'teaches' thinking as well as programming
imperative	no	mainstream general-purpose structured language of the 1970s and 1980s
imperative	no	an author language for production of computer-aided instruction materials
imperative	no	introduced new simple concepts but never gained popularity
logical	yes	artificial intelligence uses – a very different language
imperative	no	almost an applications package for producing business reports
object-oriented	yes	simulation
object-oriented	yes	forerunner of most graphics interfaces
functional	yes	string manipulation language

structure: *'imperative'* indicates that the language is used by giving instructions on how to solve the problem (an algorithm, or conventional program);
'functional' indicates that it is based on functions or procedures applied to sets of data;
'object-oriented ' indicates that the basic structure is a programming language in which types of data (*objects*) are defined with the kind of operations that can be carried out on them.

ext indicates whether or not the language is *extensible* by adding new syntax words of the programmer's choice, that are then processed in the same way as the built-in words.

Operating system

including: disk operating system, DOS, MS-DOS, UNIX, Windows
is a program or suite of programs that controls the entire operation of the computer. It is normally provided by the manufacturer and deals with the basic functions of the computer, such as detecting what has been typed in, displaying data on the screen and loading and saving to backing store. Most modern operating systems include *utility programs* (see above) which make the operation of the computer easier, such as a program to format a disk.

The portion of the operating system that deals with access to and management of files and programs stored on disk, is often provided separately. This is the *disk operating system* (commonly abbreviated to *DOS*). A *network operating system* (see page 152) provides similar facilities for use with local area networks.

Many modern operating systems also provide a *graphical user interface* (see page 71), often incorporated into the operating system.

MS-DOS is an operating system originally written for the IBM Personal Computer (IBM-PC). It is now the most common operating system used with PC-compatible microcomputers.

UNIX is an operating system originally written for large machines. Versions are now available for a variety of machines ranging from mainframes to microcomputers.

Windows is the graphical user interface developed by Microsoft for computers using the MS-DOS operating system. Many users do not need to be aware of what operating system is used as the Windows user interface appears to do most of the required system operations.
Windows 95 is a combined graphical user interface and operating system.

B11   Data Representation and Management

*This section is concerned with terms involved in the
organisation of data for manipulation and storage in a
computer system. Other related terms will be found in
sections A1 Data Processing, A2 Word Processing,
A3 Spreadsheets, A5 Databases and Information Retrieval,
B3 Memory.*

Data Representation is the coding of data in a form suitable for storing and
processing it. The essence of any computer is its ability to store and
manipulate data. Within the computer all information is represented as some
combinations of physical properties. What these properties mean depends on
how we interpret them. Indeed a particular set of these properties could
represent a number, a letter, a word, an instruction within a program or a
variety of other things. What a particular set of properties is taken to mean
depends on the context it is in when interpreted by the computer's central
processor.

   In a digital computer these properties are made up of individual elements
which can have one of two values (often voltages). It is convenient for us to
think of this element as a binary digit (a **bit**) which can be written as either 0
or 1. Binary digits can then be grouped to form patterns which are used as
codes.

   The codes allow us to describe how data is stored and manipulated in a
way which is common between computer systems. We can also consider the
codes as binary numbers which allows us to use mathematical theory to
manipulate the data.

Files are used to hold both data and programs. It is usual to keep programs
separate from the data they operate on. The data is usually held as one or
more files on backing storage, portions of which are copied into primary
storage in order to work on individual items of data. The operating systems
software does the copying between backing and primary storage, ensuring that
the correct portion is readily available. Because of this automatic management
of files, users must access files in a formal way.

   If the file is a new one, it must first be *created*, and this might include
specifying how large the file will become, and how it will be organised.

   If a file is no longer needed, it may be *deleted* from backing store so that
the space it occupies is available for other files.

Data

is information coded and structured for subsequent processing, generally by a computer system. The resulting codes are meaningless until they are placed in the correct context. The subtle difference between data and information is that information is in context, data is not.

Numeric data

is data which is intended to be interpreted and manipulated as numbers. Much of the data stored in a computer are numbers of some kind. So long as the values are not exceedingly large nor very close to zero, representing a stored value presents no problems. Because of the ways in which numbers are stored and manipulated some computer calculations will not be exact, particularly when division is used. However, the calculations performed by a computer are at least as accurate as a typical calculator. See also, *data type*, page 7.

Character data

including: character
is made up of letters, digits, spaces, punctuation marks which can be printed or displayed on a screen and other non-printing characters, such as end of paragraph indicators. These are referred to as *characters.*

Each individual character is represented by a single code number (see *character set*, below) stored as a binary integer. Data in the form of text will be stored as a sequence of these codes. See also, *data type*, page 7.

Character set

including: character code, ASCII, American Standard Code for Information Interchange, Teletext character set
is the set of symbols that may be represented by a computer at a particular time. These symbols are called *characters* (see above). Individual characters are represented by a single code number, the *character code*, stored as a binary integer. When the data is displayed or printed, the code is converted into the appropriate shape for the character. The range of characters that may be represented by a computer at any particular time is determined by the character code set in use at that time.

There are a number of character sets, most of them based on *ASCII* (*American Standard Code for Information Interchange*).

There are international standard character sets with variations for use in different cultures, for example Russian or Greek.

The *teletext character set*, used by Ceefax and Oracle, enables screen displays involving simple graphics to be constructed. These are very compact codes and can be economically transmitted.

File

including: file name extension

is a collection of related data. It is traditional to think of computer data files as being made up of a collection of identically structured *records* (see below), with each record made up of a number of *fields* (see below). Other kinds of files, such as graphics files, have different structures.

To be accessed, a file has to have a name which is recognised by the system. Disk operating systems determine the conventions for file names. All file names carry some kind of extension, *file name extension*, which may or may not be user controlled. The file name extension identifies the kind of data in the file, for example graphic data, word processed document. See also *file type*, below.

Record

including: record format, fixed-length record, fixed-format record, variable-length record

is the basic unit of data stored in a datafile. It is a collection of items, which may be of different *data types* (see page 7), all relating to an individual or object that the record describes. A record is treated as a single unit for processing. Most datafiles contain records which have the same types of information but about different individuals or objects.

The contents of a record are described by the *record format* which specifies the record in terms of its *fields* (see below). The records in a file may designed to have either fixed or variable length.

The length of a *fixed-length record* (or *fixed-format record*) is decided at the design stage. This length is often thought of in terms of a number of characters and cannot be changed later.

The length of a *variable-length record* is governed by the amount of data (the number of characters) to be stored.

Variable-length records are useful where textual data is to be stored, which would leave a lot of wasted space in fixed-length records. However fixed-length records are more easily processed.

Field

including: field name

is part of a *record* (see above) designed to hold a single data item of a specified type. Most datafiles contain records which have the same fields of information but about different individuals or objects. Each field is referred to by a *field name*, which identifies the data in the field and makes it possible to generalise about the data being processed. Figure B11.1 (below) shows the use of records and a file.

FIELDS AND RECORDS

A **datafile** *holding details of club membership.*

Each **record** *would contain* **fields** *of a member's data:*

> *name, initials, date of birth and membership number.*

The **field names:**

> **Name, Initials, Date_Of_Birth** *and* **Membership_Number**

identify the data present, rather than being the actual data, which may be:

> **Smith, F, 12/3/78, 458923**

Each **record** *would have the name, initials, date of birth and membership number of a different member.*

Figure B11.1: Fields and records in a datafile

Key

including: key field, sort key, primary key, key field order, secondary key, composite key

is the field (the *key field*) within a record used to identify the record, for example a bank account number identifies a customer's account. The key can be used for finding the record within a file or as the *sort key* for sorting a file into order.

Most datafiles will have a *primary key*, which is unique and used to identify the record. If the records in a datafile can be accessed *sequentially* (see *sequential access*, below) the records will be accessed in *key field order*, which is the order they will be in when they have been sorted using the key field.

Datafiles may also have *secondary keys*, which enable the file to be accessed in a different order. *Composite keys*, made up of more than one field, can be used to sort a file. The use of composite keys is shown in Figure B11.2.

KEY FIELDS

In the example (Figure B11.1) of a datafile holding details of club membership containing **fields** *for:*

Name, Initials, Date_Of_Birth *and* **Membership_Number**

The **Membership_Number** *could be the* **primary key** *field because it is unique and identifies who the record is about.*

Name *could be a* **secondary key**.

Date_Of_Birth *or* **Initials** *could <u>not</u> be* **key** *fields because without the other fields they are out of context (and the data is unidentifiable and meaningless).*

Date_Of_Birth *could be a* **sort key** *because the resulting list would be in order of age, which is useful.*

Name *and* **Initials** *(i.e.* **Smith F**) *could be a* **composite key**.

If the file is sorted using this as a sort key, *all the* **Smiths** *would be together, in alphabetic order according to* **initial**.

Figure B11.2: Key fields in a datafile

Sort

is to arrange data items in order (for example, alphabetical or numerical). When the data items are themselves structured, one part of the structure has to be used in determining the ordering. In a file of names and addresses, for example, the 'surname' might be used for the ordering. See also *key*, above.

File operations

including: open, close, read, write, update, insert, append, read-only
are those activities that can be performed on an existing data file.

Before a file can be used it is necessary to *open* the file. All or part of the file will be copied to main memory. Any changes will be made to this copy and in due course written back to the file in backing store. If access is requested to a part of the file not currently in main memory, the operating system is responsible for loading a copy of the required portion of the file. When access to a file is no longer needed, it must be *closed* so that changes are written back to the permanent version stored on backing store.

Reading is the operation of taking a copy of a data item from a file.
Writing is the operation of saving any changes to a file.
Updating is altering an existing data item already written in the file.
Inserting is adding a new data item to an existing file. This implies moving all later items to make space.
Appending is adding a new item at the end of an existing file.

In multi-user systems, problems can arise if more than one user is allowed to access a file at any one time. Only the first user who requests access to a file will be allowed to update it or append to it. Until the first user has released the file, subsequent requests for access may be denied or allowed only to read the file or individual records (*read-only* access).

Merge

is to combine two or more data files into a single file. These files must have the same structure and have been sorted in the same way, for example alphabetically. The merged file has the same structure as the original files and is ordered in the same way. See also *sort*, *key* and *field*, above.

Export

including: import
is to create a data file using one piece of software, so that it can be read by another piece of software. The software that reads the 'exported' file is said to be *importing* it.

File access

including: serial access, sequential access, direct access, index sequential access, ISAM
is the process of obtaining data from a file. The way in which a file is to be accessed determines how it is stored, and what information the systems software needs to hold in order to achieve efficient reading and writing.

Methods of file access include:

Serial access: items are read, one record at a time, from the start of the file in the order in which they are stored.

Sequential access: items are read, one record at a time, in the *key field order*, as if the file were arranged in key field order (see *key*, above).

Direct access: any item can be retrieved immediately, provided its position in the file is known. This often means that items must have a known length, so that software can calculate where to find the required item.

Index Sequential Access Methods (**ISAM**) use a sequential file with an index of the records. Both the file and the index are in alphabetic order. When searching an index sequential file of surnames to locate 'Smith', the index is first consulted to find the first item beginning with 'S', then the file is searched sequentially from this point onwards.

Validation

also known as: data vetting

including: range check, check digit, verification, batch total, control total, check sum

is computerised checking to detect any data that is unreasonable or incomplete. There are many methods of validation, designed to suit the data being processed.

Some validation processes operate on single data items:

a *range check* should identify any data items outside a plausible range (such as a worker's age that was less than 15, or over 75, perhaps);

a *check digit* is an extra digit placed at the end of a numeric data item (such as a bank account number): the check digit is calculated from the other digits in a way that can be repeated for checking the data.

Other methods cross check between data items.

Verification is checking the transfer of data into or within a computer systemby comparing copies of the data before and after transfer. For keyboard input see *data verification,* page 5.

Other methods operate on batches of data:

a *batch total* of the number of separate records in a batch might be manually calculated and added to the data, as a check that none had been missed;

a *control total* formed by adding up some field from each record could accompany the batch as a double-check.

Where the data is computer software, a *check sum* formed by simply adding up all the instructions, treated as numbers, is often put at the end of the file to provide a check that it has been copied without error.

File type

including: CSV file (Comma Separated Variable file), TSV file (Tab Separated Variable file), SID file (Standard Interchangeable Data file), RTF file (Revisable Text Format file or Rich Text Format file), ASCII file, text file is the labelling of a file to identify the structure of its contents. This means that the user knows which software can be used with that data and that an applications program knows how to load and interpret the data. In some cases the operating system uses the file type to locate, load and run the application software as well. The *file name extension* (see above) often indicates the file type.

Most application programs have their own file types for data stored in their format. Other file types are used to transfer data between applications. Some common file types are detailed below:

CSV (*Comma Separated Variable*) *files* have each field separated by a comma, in addition each field may be enclosed in quotation marks to avoid ambiguity. CSV files are used to transfer tabular data, that is data held in the form of tables, between applications.

TSV (*Tab Separated Variable*) *files* have each field separated by a special character (the tab character) to avoid ambiguity. TSV files are also used to transfer tabular data between applications.

SID (*Standard Interchangeable Data*) *files* have a format which allows tabular and other data to be stored. SID files are used to transfer tabular and some other types of data between applications. SID files are not commonly used outside software designed for the UK education market.

RTF (*Revisable Text Format* or *Rich Text Format*) *files* have a complex format for storing word processor data, including information about fonts, sizes, colour and styles. This standard file format can be used to transfer data between most word processor packages without losing the formatting information.

ASCII or *Text files* hold the data only as individual characters in the standard ASCII code. See *character set*, above. No formatting information is included and, as a result, ASCII or text files are acceptable to many different applications and provide one of the most common means of transferring textual data between application packages. Most packages that allow data to be *imported* (see *import*, below) will accept a text file.

Corruption

is the introduction of errors into data or programs during storage or copying. It is usually due to physical causes, such as electrical interference or faulty equipment.

Download

including: upload

is to transfer data or programs from a larger computer (such as a mainframe) to a smaller one (such as a personal computer). The reverse process is called *uploading.*

Data compression

is the technique of reducing the space occupied by a large file. There are many different methods, suited to different types of data. For example: the first paragraph of the introduction to this section (B11 Data Representation and Management), contains 611 characters, including spaces; it can be reduced in size, without losing any of the information it contains, by replacing certain common pairs of letters by a single character (we have illustrated this by using numbers). For example, there are 12 occurrences of the pair 'th'. If these are replaced by '0', 12 characters have been saved. Making the changes listed in Figure B11.1, the paragraph is reduced to 507 characters, a saving of 104 characters or about 17%. The file must be re-expanded before it can be used, of course, but space has been saved in storage. See also *video data compression*, page 132.

DATA COMPRESSION

D7a 1p1sent7io4i2o3codi5 of d7a i4a form suitabl3for stori586 processi5 it . o3essenc3of8ny comput9 i2it2ability to sto186 manipul73d7a. Wi0i403co mput98ll inform7io4i21p1sented82som3combin7ion2of physical prop9ties. Wh7 0es3prop9tie2mea4depe62o4how w3int9p1t 0em. I6eed8 particular se t of 0es3prop9tie2could 1p1sent8 numb9,8 lett9,8 word,84instructio4wi0i4 a program or8 variety of o09 0i5s. Wh78 particular set of prop9tie2i2take4t o mea4depe62o403context it i2i4whe4int9p1ted by 03comput9'2central pro cessor.

Replacements:
0 = th	1 = re	2 = s'N'	3 = e'N'	4 = n'N'
5 = ng	6 = nd	7 = at	8 = 'N'a	9 = er

(a space is represented by 'N')

Figure B11.1: A simple example of data compression

Part C:
APPENDICES

One characteristic of modern life, and particularly any form of technological activity, is the use of abbreviations, acronyms and other 'jargon' by those who are involved in any specialised activity. This use of words, terms and acronyms when writing for or talking to others involved in the same activity can be a way of economically passing information between like minded people, but on the other hand it can also be a barrier to understanding for those who do not know the meanings of the strange new words. Computer users have always made great use of a vocabulary containing many abbreviations and acronyms.

In section C1 there is a list of some acronyms and abbreviations that may be encountered by users of this glossary. The list is alphabetic and does not include any terms to be found in the main body of the glossary, which can be found by looking in the index. The information provided is the expansion of the acronym and, for some terms, an indication (in brackets) of the context in which they may be met.

C1   *Acronyms and Abbreviations*

This alphabetic list of acronyms and abbreviations contains some of the more important ones not included in the definitions in this glossary. Sometimes brackets are used to indicate the context in which the acronym or abbreviation may be met.

ACM	Association for Computing Machinery
ADC	analog-to-digital converter
AFIPS	American Federation of Information Processing Societies
ALU	arithmetic logic unit
AM	amplitude modulation (communications)
ANSI	American National Standards Institute
ATM	asynchronous transfer mode (communications)
BABT	British Approvals Board for Telecommunications
BCD	binary coded decimal
BCS	British Computer Society
BDOS	basic disk operating system
BEAB	British Electrical Appliances Board
BIOS	basic input output system
BNF	Bachus-Naur form
BPP	bits per pixel
BSI	British Standards Institution
CAI	computer assisted instruction
CASE	computer aided software engineering
CCA	Central Computing Agency
CCITT	Committée Consultatif International Téléphonique et Télégraphique
CD-I	compact disc interactive
CEG	Computer Education Group
CEPIS	Confederation of European Professional Informatics Societies
CISC	complex instruction set computer
CP/M or	control program monitor or
CPM	control program for microcomputers
CROM	control ROM
CRT	cathode ray tube
CTRL or Ctrl	control (ASCII character)
CWP	communicating word processors
DAC	digital-to-analog converter
DAT	digital audio tape
DBA	database administrator

DEL	delete (keyboard)
DIN	Deutsche Industrienorm
DMA	direct-memory access
DML	data manipulation language
EA	extended addressing
EBCDIC	extended binary coded decimal interchange code
ECMA	European Computer Manufacturers Association
EIA	Electrical Industries Association (USA)
EISA	extended industry standard architecture
EPOS	electronic point-of-sale terminal
ESC	escape (keyboard)
FAM	fast access memory
FFT	fast fourier transform
FIFO	first in, first out
FSM	frequency shift modulation
FTP	file transfer protocol (communications)
Gb	giga byte
GIGO	garbage-in garbage-out
GND	ground (connection)
HDTV	high definition television
HEX	hexadecimal
Hz	Hertz
IC	integrated circuit
IEE	Institution of Electrical Engineers (UK)
IEEE	Institute of Electronic and Electrical Engineers (USA)
IFIP	International Federation for Information Processing
IR	infra red
IS	information systems
ISD	international subscriber dialling
ISO	International Standards Organisation
ISR	interrupt service routine
JSD	Jackson structured design
JSP	Jackson structure programming
Kb	kilo-bit, kilo-byte
LIFO	last in, first out
LPT	(line) printer
LSI	large-scale integration
Mb	mega byte
MDR	memory data register
MIPS	million instructions per second
MOS	metal-oxide-semiconductor
MOS	machine operating system
MPS	microprocessor system
ms	millisecond
MSD	most significant digit

MSI	medium-scale integration
MTBF	mean time before failure
MUX	multiplexor
ns	nanosecond
NTSC	National Television Standards Committee (USA)
NUL	null (do nothing)
OLE	object linking and embedding
OOD	object oriented design
OOL	object oriented language
OOP	object oriented program/programming
OSI	Open Systems Interchange
OV	overflow
PCB	printed circuit board
PCI	programmable communications interface
PCMCIA	personal computer memory card international association
PIO	parallel input/output
ppm	pages per minute
PRN	printer
PSN	packet switching network
PSS	packet switching system
PSTN	Public Switched Telephone Network
PSU	power supply unit
PTO	public telephone operator
QBE	query by example
QIC	quarter-inch cartridge
RDMS or RDBMS	relational database management system
REM	remark(s)
RF	radio frequency
RFI	radio frequency interference
RI	ring in
RISC	reduced instruction set computer
R/W	read/write
SHF	super high frequency
SIC	silicon integrated circuit
SIMS	Schools Information Management System
SIO	serial input/output (controller)
SLSI	super large-scale integration
SMTP	simple mail transport protocol (networks)
SOS	silicon on sapphire
SQA	software quality assurance
SQL	structured query language
SSADM	Structured Systems Analysis and Design Methodology
SSI	small-scale integration
STD	subscriber trunk dialling
Tab	tabulation (keyboard)

TCP	transmission control protocol (networks)
TCP/IP	transmission control protocol/internet protocol (networks)
TEMP	temporary
TP	teleprocessing
TP	transaction processing
TPI	tracks per inch
TRL	transistor-resistor logic
UART	universal asynchronous receiver/transmitter
UHF	ultra high frequency
UPS	uninterruptable power supply
USART	universal synchronous/asynchronous receiver/transmitter
USRT	universal synchronous receiver/transmitter
UV	ultra violet
VDG	video display generator
VDT	video display terminal
VDU	visual display unit
VESA	Video Electronics Standards Association
VHF	very high frequency
VLSI	very large-scale integration
WR	write
WS	working store
4GL	fourth generation language

C2   UNITS

Symbol	Prefix	Meaning	Decimal	Power of ten
T	tera	one million million	1 000 000 000 000	10^{12}
G	giga	one thousand million	1 000 000 000	10^{9}
M	mega	one million	1 000 000	10^{6}
K	kilo	one thousand	1 000	10^{3}
		one	1	10
m	milli	one thousandth (1/1 000)	0. 001	$10^{-3} = 1/10^{3}$
μ	micro	one millionth (1/1 000 000)	0. 000 001	$10^{-6} = 1/10^{6}$
n	nano	one thousand-millionth (1/1 000 000 000)	0. 000 000 001	$10^{-9} = 1/10^{9}$
p	pico	one million-millionth (1/1 000 000 000 000)	0.000 000 000 001	$10^{-12} = 1/10^{12}$

In computer storage terms, the symbols K, M, G and T have particular values related to the powers of 2, not to the powers of 10:

K is $2^{10} = 1\,024$, thus 8Kb (8 Kilo-bytes) of store is $8 \times 2^{10} = 8\,192$ bytes

M is $2^{20} = 1\,048\,576$, thus 4Mb (4 Mega-bytes) is $4 \times 2^{20} = 4\,194\,304$ bytes

G is $2^{30} = 1\,073\,741\,824$, thus 60Gb (60 Giga-bytes) is $60 \times 2^{30} =$
$$64\,424\,509\,440 \text{ bytes}$$

T is $2^{40} = 1\,099\,511\,627\,776$, thus 2Tb (2 Tera-bytes) is $2 \times 2^{40} =$
$$2\,199\,023\,255\,552 \text{ bytes}$$

Index